AF566783

Training of Human Processes

Training of Human Processes

Sushama Khanna
Dean & Director (Outreach)
Udai Pareek HR-LABS,
EMPI Business School,
New Delhi

Ane Books Pvt. Ltd.
New Delhi ♦ Chennai ♦ Mumbai
Bengaluru ♦ Kolkata ♦ Thiruvananthapuram ♦ Lucknow

Training of Human Processes

Sushama Khanna

Published by

Ane Books Pvt. Ltd.
4821, Parwana Bhawan, 1st Floor, 24 Ansari Road,
Darya Ganj, **New Delhi** - 110 002, India
Tel.: +91(011) 23276843-44, Fax: +91(011) 23276863
e-mail: kapoor@anebooks.com, Website: www.anebooks.com

Branches

- Avantika Niwas, 1st Floor, 19 Doraiswamy Road, T. Nagar, **Chennai** - 600 017, Tel.: +91(044) 28141554, 28141209 e-mail: anebooks_tn@airtelmail.in
- Plot No. 59, Sector-1, Shirwane, Nerul, **Navi Mumbai** - 400 706, Tel.: +91(022) 27720842, 27720851 e-mail: anebooksmum@mtnl.net.in
- 38/1, 1st Floor, Model House, First Street, Opp. Shamanna Park, Basavannagudi, **Bengaluru** - 560 004, Tel.: +91(080) 41681432, 26620045 e-mail: anebang@airtelmail.in
- Flat No. 16A, 220 Vivekananda Road, Maniktalla, **Kolkata** - 700 006, Tel.: +91(033) 23547119, 23523639 e-mail: anebooks_vsn@bsnl.in
- # 6, TC 25/2710, Kohinoor Flats, Lukes Lane, Ambujavilasam Road, **Thiruvananthapuram** - 01, Kerala, Tel.: +91(0471) 4068777, 4068333 e-mail: anebookstvm@airtelmail.in

Representative Office

- C-26, Sector-A, Mahanagar, **Lucknow** - 226 006 Mobile - +91 93352 29971

ISBN (10) : 81-8052-245-8
ISBN (13) : 978-81-8052-245-1

Printed at : Gopaljee Enterprises, Delhi.

Foreword

Kurt Lewin laid the foundations for "Laboratory Education" in the US which subsequently spread to the rest of the world. Laboratory education deals with "Creating" experiences in various "Settings" and learning from them. The experiences are created in settings ranching from two person transactions to society at large. In two person situations role plays, negotiation, communication, empathy, listening, understanding etc., various skills can be exhibited, tested, practiced and learnt. In community settings various alternate methods or interventions can be used and their impact in producing desired change can be studied. Often these interventions done in a planned way to study the effects are called 'action research'. In organisational setting they are often referred to as OD/interventions. Of all the settings, the most experimented are group-settings. Laboratory education using groups has become most used settings. This is because groups are an important component in organisations as well as society. Studying behaviour of people in groups as well as studying group behaviour has become a significant focal point of research. Small groups have been found to offer ideal settings for learning about individual behaviour and experimenting with the same.

Kurt Lewin's T-Group technology (also known as L-Group technology or sensitivity training) was introduced to India by Stalwarts in the field like Dr Udai Pareek, Dr Somnath Chattopadhyay, Francis Menizzer, Suresh Srivastava, Ishwar Dayal, Late Nitish De, Dr Dharni Sinha etc. in early sixties. In sixties State Bank of India and many other corporations made them an integral part of their training. Seeing the success of laboratory education through T-Groups or L-Groups the above mentioned stalwarts created a not for profit society called ISABS in early seventies to promote laboratory education. Recently EMPI has institutionalised the same by starting Udai Pareek, HR Labs.

I am happy that Dr. Sushama Khanna took pains to document some of the process in this book. There are very few such documents in India towards this goal. I congratulate Sushama for making this contribution to the world of Indian Behavioural Science. I am sure the students and other readers will find this a great book to read.

T. V. Rao
Chairman, T V R L S,
Former President, ISABS

Preface

Organisations, in order to be successful, need to place a high priority on proactivity and systematic understanding of organisational issues and on responding to current and future external customer needs. Workforce mobility and diversity are creating new employee needs along with new expectations about the work culture, and these needs, too, have to be systematically understood and responded to. Although technology is important, but people are more important, since technology can not work without the involvement of people. For organisations or societies to grow, it is very important to understand human processes like motivation, communication, decision making, leadership, etc. HR leaders are challenged to become effective strategic partners in the creation of world class learning culture.

There has been a revolutionary change in the Human Resource field in the last one decade. Experiential training is being recognised and considered more effective way of learning human processes. One of the most important of these is the recognition of *Laboratory Training* for strategic development. In India, O.D. and planned change started in the early 1960s. A group of Indian professionals trained at the National Training Laboratories (NTL) at Bethel, Maine, USA, brought out a good deal of O.D. technology in India. Grid programs were initiated and widely used in the Small Industries Extension Training (SIET) Institute, Hyderabad, State Bank of India and in the Indian Institute of Management (IIM) programs in the mid-1960s. Unfortunately these remained isolated efforts and did not take O.D. to its logical conclusions.

In the mid-1970s, O.D. was first introduced in India in Larsen and Toubro as a formal and structured part of the HRD department. It was expected that the change process would get institutionalised and more O.D. and process specialists would be developed. Unfortunately, this did not happen as the corporate sector in the country has a very protected and secure environment and there were very few compulsions to change. Hence, O.D. remained mostly in academic institutions - the forte of a few specialists and largely limited to T-Group training and other training based interventions. That it has a slow growth is indicated by the fact that even after 25 years of existence, the Indian Society for Applied Behavioural Science (ISABS), an associate of NTL, produced less than 200 process specialists in the vast country.

Laboratory Training has been a major component in the growth of organisational development and management education. T-Group technology is inherent in the teaching of managerial skills, interpersonal skills, self-awareness, diversity and group dynamics. Laboratory Training was a great training innovation which provided the base for team building. This was a new method that would help leaders and managers create a more humanistic, people serving system and allow leaders and managers to see how their behavior actually affected others. There was a strong value of concern for people and a desire to create systems that took people's needs and feelings seriously.

T-Group is designed to help each individual realize his own potential growth more fully and to increase his ability to work effectively with others in a variety of situations. By learning how to develop effective teamwork, individuals can join forces to bring about organisational and community change and improvement. The group's work is primarily process rather than content oriented. The focus tends to be on the feelings and the communication of feelings, rather than on the communication of information, opinions, or concepts. This is accomplished by focusing on the 'here and now' behaviour in the group. Attention is paid to particular behaviours of participants not on the "whole person", feedback is non-evaluative and reports on the impact of the behaviour on others. The participant has the opportunity to become a more authentic self in relation to others through self-disclosure and receiving feedback from others.

The present volume has largely emerged out of need for the students of HR-LABS, when we introduced a course in *Human Processes* in 1994. In 1994, Pankaj Saran, Vice President, EMPI, who is constantly questioning various systems, questioned the relevance of HR courses carried out by various educational institutes for the relevance to the organisations. He contacted few like minded professionals and as a result *Human Resource Laboratory for Applied Behavioral Sciences (HR-LABS*) emerged under the chairmanship of Dr. Udai Pareek. It was decided that a post graduate program would be especially designed to match the organizational requirement. The program would be mainly experiential and would be based on applied psychology and behavioural sciences. It was decided to include human processes lab as part of curricula.

We named this *Human Resource Laboratory for Applied Behavioural Sciences* for a good reason. The major method of learning employed at HR-LABS is one in which students are helped to diagnose and experiment with their own behaviour, students are both experimenters and subjects in a joint learning activities. Faculty serves as guides in institulization of experimental and collaborative approaches to learning at HR-LABS. They also guide students in the transfer of learning outside in various organisational settings.

Laboratory and T-Group methods have increasingly been incorporated into the program, *Post Graduate Program in Human Resource and Organisational Development (PGPHR&OD)*. When we looked for a comprehensive book in human processes, we found none. The purpose of the book is to share concerns, experiences, and thinking on a vital subject. The book starts with introduction, moves on to group processes, and finally talks about some conceptual discussions, and ends by integrating thinking and work into one effective thread.

Present volume has been divided into three sections. First part gives introduction to human processes, their importance, and effective way of training human resources. It also talks about the laboratory methods or T-Groups for the training of human resources. Part two discusses some of Individual and Group Processes like Group Norms, Giving and Receiving Feedback, Sympathy versus Empathy, Thinking versus Feeling, etc. part three discusses theories of human resources like Johari Window, Transactional Analysis, Emotional Intelligence etc.

I hope that the book will motivate my students and my other colleagues of ISABS to share their experiences, and comment on the conceptual framework and scheme used in this volume, and propose alternative ones to illustrate their experiences. I have provided the minimum material to stimulate thinking, and to encourage innovative approaches in T-Group. If I am able to communicate this enthusiasm and optimism to the readers, who may be enthused to enrich their knowledge regarding T-Group, I shall regard my effort more than rewarded.

New Delhi **Sushama Khanna**

Contents

List of Exhibits

Part One

Introduction

1. **Training Human Processes through Laboratory Methods**
2. **Life of a Group**
3. **Dynamics of Silence in T-Group**
4. **"Are T-Group Experiences Applicable in Real World"**
5. **How to Write a Personal Journal**

Chapter 1

Training Human Processes through Laboratory Methods

> *"Learning is more effective when it is an active rather than a passive process."*
>
> **– Kurt Lewin**

Technology has been changing very fast, but human beings are the same for centuries. They still have the same emotions, same personal and interpersonal issues. The fast changing technology has affected many aspects of human life and as a result organisations, communities and society at large are also affected. In this context, importance of human processes has increased tremendously. It is easy to buy technology, but impossible to buy human processes like motivation, communication, decision-making, leadership, interpersonal relationships, effective negotiation, etc. Understanding human dynamics has become not only important, but crucial for the survival of organisations and societies.

An effective way of accelerating learning, training and understanding human processes is a use of laboratory methods, popularly called T-Groups or Learning Groups. The T-Group was a great training innovation which provided the base for what we now know about team building. This was a new method that would help leaders and managers create a more humanistic, people serving system and allow leaders and managers to see how their behaviour actually affected others. There was a strong value of concern for people and a desire to create systems that took people's needs and feelings seriously.

A T-Group (Training Group) is facilitated experiential learning, focused on the here and now, in an unstructured small group setting. It is also known as Sensitivity Training or L-Group (Learning group). It was invented in the late 1940's by Kurt Lewin, Ken Benne, Leland Bradford and Ronald Lippitt, and was the basis for the founding of the National Training Laboratory for the Applied Behavioural Sciences in Bethel, ME, USA in 1947. They pioneered the use of T-Groups (Laboratory Training) in which the learners use "here and now" experience in the group, feedback among participants and theory on human behaviour to explore group process and gain insights into themselves and others. The goal is to offer people options for their behaviour in groups.

A Description

The T-Group provides participants with an opportunity to learn about themselves, their impact on others and how to function more effectively in group and interpersonal situations. It facilitates this learning by bringing together a small group of people (10 –12) for the purpose of studying their own behaviour when they interact within a small group. A T-Group is not a group discussion or a problem solving group.

The group's work is primarily process rather than content oriented. The focus tends to be on the feelings and the communication of feelings, rather than on the communication of information, opinions, or concepts. This is accomplished by focusing on the 'here and now' behaviour in the group. Attention is paid to particular behaviours of participants not on the "whole person", feedback is non-evaluative and reports on the impact of the behaviour on others. The participant has the opportunity to become a more authentic self in relation to others through self-disclosure and receiving feedback from others. The Johari Window is a model that looks at that process.

The training is not structured in the manner you might experience in an academic program or a meeting with an agenda or a team with a task to accomplish. The lack of structure and limited involvement of the trainers provides space for the participants to decide what they want to talk about. No one tells them what they ought to talk about. The lack of direction results in certain characteristic responses; participants are silent or aggressive or struggle to start discussions or attempt to structure the group.

In the beginning of a T-Group participants are usually focused on what they experience as a need for structure, individual emotional safety, predictability, and something to do in common. These needs are what amount to the tip of the iceberg in most groups in their back home situation. By not filling the group's time with answers to these needs, the T-Group eventually begins to notice what is under the tip of the iceberg. It is, what is always there in any group but often unseen and ignored. So, participants experience anxiety about authority and power, being included and being accepted in the group, and intimacy.

Depending on forces, such as, the dynamics of the group, the past experience and competence of participants, and the skill of the trainers—the group, to some extent, usually develops a sense of itself as a group, with feelings of group loyalty. This can cause groups to resist learning opportunities if they are seen as threatening to the group's self-image. It also provides climate of trust, support and permission needed for individuals to try new behaviour.

As an individual participant begins to experience some degree of trust (in himself, the group and the trainers) several things become possible—

- The participant may notice that his/her feelings and judgments about the behaviour of others are not always shared by others. That what he/she found supportive or threatening was not experienced in that way by others in the group. That how one responded to authority, acceptance and affection issues are different from that of others (more related to ones family of origin than to what is happening in the group). Individual differences emerge in how experiences are understood.

- The participant may begin to try on new behaviour. For example, someone who has always felt a need to fill silence with noise and activity tries being quieter and still.
- Participants begin to ask for feedback from the group about how their behaviour is impacting others.

  Participants may find that they are really rather independent and have a relatively low level of anxiety about what is happening in the group. They exhibit a broader range of behaviour and emotions during the life of the group. In fact their leadership is part of what helps the group.

Objectives of T-Group Learning

- Human relations laboratory training is designed to help each individual realise his own potential growth more fully and to increase his ability to work effectively with others in a variety of situations. By learning how to develop effective teamwork, individuals can join forces to bring about organisational and community change and improvement. The following factors are seen as important broad objectives of training:
- Self-insight.
- Better understanding of other persons and increased skill in achieving group effectiveness.
- Increased recognition of the characteristics of larger social systems.
- Greater awareness of the dynamics of change.
- Increased understanding of group development and dynamics.
- Increased interpersonal skills.
- Increased ability to experiment with their behaviour.
- Increased awareness of own feelings in the moment; and offer the opportunity to accept responsibility for own feelings.
- Increased sensitivity to others' feelings.
- Increased ability to give and receive feedback.

- Increased ability to learn from their own and a group's experience.
- Increased ability to manage and utilise conflict.
- Increased understanding of the impact of their behaviour on others.
- Increased understanding of process in the small group.

Success in these goals depends, to a large extent, on the implied contract that each participant is willing to disclose feelings that she or he may have, in the moment, about others in the group, and to solicit feedback from the others about herself or himself. The focus is upon individual learning; some participants may learn a great deal in most of the above areas, others learn relatively little.

Sources of Change in Groups

- *Self-observation :* Participants give more attention to their own intentions, feelings, etc.
- *Feedback :* Participants receive information on the impact they have on others.
- *Insight :* Participants expand self-knowledge.
- *Self-disclosure :* Participants expose more of themselves to others.
- *Universality :* Participants experience that others share their difficulties, concerns or hopes.
- *Group Cohesion :* Participants experience trust, acceptance and understanding.
- *Hope :* Participants see others learn, achieve their goals, improve, and cope more effectively
- *Vicarious Learning :* Participants pick up skills and attitudes from others.
- *Catharsis :* Participants experience a sense of release or breakthrough by disclosure.

Essentials for Laboratory Learning

Certain conditions need to be met in various ways if participants are to reach personal goals of improvement and change in insights, understandings, sensitivities and skills, as given below:

1. **Presentation of self :** Until the individual has an opportunity to reveal the way he sees things and does things, he has little basis for improvement and change.
2. **Feedback:** Individuals do not learn from their experience. They learn from bringing out the essential patterns of purposes, motives and behaviour in a situation where they can receive back clear and accurate information about the relevancy and effectiveness of their behaviour. They need a feedback system which continuously operates so that they can change and correct what is inappropriate?
3. **Atmosphere:** An atmosphere of trust and non-defensiveness is necessary for people both to be willing to expose their behaviour and purposes and to accept feedback.
4. **Cognitive map:** Knowledge from research theory and experience is important and needed to enable the individual, both to understand his experiences and to generalise from them. But generally information is most effective when it follows experience and feedback.
5. **Experience:** Unless there is opportunity to try out new patterns of thoughts and behaviour. They never become a part of the individuals. Without experimental efforts relevant change is difficult to make.
6. **Practice:** Equally important is the need to practice new approaches so that the individual gains security in being different.
7. **Application:** Unless learning and change can be applied to back home situations, they are not likely to be effective or lasting. Attention needs to be given to helping individuals plan application.
8. **Relearning — "How to learn":** Since much of our academic experience has led us to believe that we learn out of listening to authorities, there is rarely a need to learn how to learn from presentation of self, feedback and experimentation. So the T-Group experience provides opportunities to explore traditional patterns of behaviour.

Expected Outcomes of a T-Group

1. Unfreezing habitual responses to situations — this is facilitated by the participant's own desire to explore new ways of behaving and the trainer staying non-directive, silent, and providing little structure or task agenda.

2. Self-generated and chosen change by the participant – Experiment with new behaviours –Practice description not evaluation of behaviour.

3. Reinforcement of new behaviour by receiving positive feedback, participant's own assessment of whether what is happening is closer to what she/he intends, supportive environment and trust development.

A training laboratory tries to create a climate encouraging learnings, understandings, insights, skills in the areas of self, group and organisation. *See* Exhibit 1.1.

Exhibit 1.1 : Learning in T-Group

Self	***Interpersonal and Group Relations***	***Organisation***
Understanding own feeling and motivations.	Establishing meaningful interpersonal relationships.	Understanding organisational complexities.
Correctly perceiving effects of behaviour of self on others.	Finding a satisfying place in the group.	Developing and inventing appropriate new patterns and procedures.
Correctly understanding effect of other's behaviour on self.	Understanding dynamic complexities in group behaviour.	Helping to diagnose and solve problems between units of the organisation.
Learning others' opinion and accepting helpful feedback and criticism.	Developing diagnostic skills to understand group problems and processes.	Working as a member and as a leader.
Appropriately interacting with others.	Acquiring skills of helping the group on task and maintenance problems.	

The Role of the Trainers

- To help the group and individuals analyze and learn from what is happening in the group. The trainer may draw attention to events and behaviour in the group and invite the group to look at its experience. At times the trainer may offer tentative interpretations.
- To offer theory, a model or research that seems related to what the group is looking at.
- To encourage the group to follow norms that tend to serve the learning process, *e.g.*, focusing on "here and now" rather than the "then and there".
- To offer training and coaching in skills that tend to help the learning process, *e.g.*, feedback skills.
- To not offer structure or an agenda. To remain silent, allowing the group to experience its anxiety about acceptance, influence, *etc.*
- To be willing to disclose oneself, to be open with the group. On occasion being willing to offer feedback and challenge a participant
- To avoid becoming too directive, clinical, or personally involved.

Possible Problem in Using T-Group Learning in Back-home Situations

T-Group methods usually encourage self-disclosure and openness, which may be inappropriate or even punished in organisations. When managers thought they could take the T-Group method into the back home organisation, they discovered that the methods and the assumptions of a T-Group did not fit. T-Groups consisted of participants who were strangers. They did not have a history or a future together and could more easily focus on *here and now* behaviour. Another issue was that in the organisation there were objectives, deadlines and schedules related to accomplishing the work of the company or group. Groups with a task to accomplish could not take the same time that would be used in a T-Group. These difficulties helped and lead to the development of Organisation Development and team building. What had been learned in T-Groups was combined with other knowledge and these new disciplines emerged as ways to address the values raised by the T-Group experience.

The T-Group experience can open up a web of questioning in a participant. Ways of behaving that the person has used for many years may be called into question by others in the group and oneself. This has in some cases brought the participant to question relationships in the family or at work. While this can be a very constructive process that leads to the renewal of relationships, it has on occasion lead to the breakdown of a relationship. While such a breakdown may have, in time, come to the relationship without participation in a T-Group, it remains a painful and possibly damaging experience.

Participants being forced or pressured to attend, by an employer or other person with influence, are on the whole less likely to have a positive learning experience. Employers or others who want to require the participation of others may enhance the chance of having a productive outcome if—they attend a lab themselves before sending others; they speak with the lab coordinator before the event to discuss what might realistically be expected and what the leader could do to assist in the learning process when the participant returns home.

❑❑❑

Chapter 2

Life of a Group

> *"Individual commitment to a group effort — that is what makes a team work, a company work, a society work, a civilisation work."*
>
> **— Vince Lombardi**
> **American Football Coach**

In the life of a group there are certain critical issues confronting it and resolutions must be found. Frequently, we find these issues are dealt with habitual ways carried over from one group situation to another without testing their appropriateness. While the training group is set up as a laboratory group for learning objectives, it too must face these same issues. In effect, the T-Group is an exciting opportunity for participants to test their habitual assumptions and behaviours and to experiment with new ones. Some of the important issues are:

Membership: Each member must find answers in group; situations as to what his roles will be. How much am I committed to give of myself? What do I want to give to others? What feelings do I have about others and about their relationships to me?

Organisation: People must organise in groups to meet various needs but the question as to what kind of organisation is most effective for the attainment of significant learning experiences is ever present in the training group. Very often we carry over procedures for prior experiences which can be tested in the ST-Group and modified or abandoned as we seek for more appropriate procedures.

Authority: What type of control in the group is necessary? What can we realistically expect by way of direction from those who have authority? Certainly just as important – what are my own feelings toward authority, toward those who are in positions of authority, and those who may be seeking authority? How appropriate are these feelings?

Data Gathering: Every group must obtain information in dealing with its problems. The kind of data will be determined by the objectives of the group. In the T-Group there is a rich source of data in terms of the ideas, feelings and perceptions of group members which if properly utilised can help the group in achieving its goals.

Learning how to learn: Frequently we find groups that exist over a long period of time but show little improvement in their ability to work more successfully in achieving group goals. In the T-Group we have an excellent opportunity not just to meet the issues confronting our group and to find some way of resolving them. We can learn a way to deal more effectively with these issues when they confront us in other groups. The person who has begun to experience the process of learning how to learn is the one who can make the training experience a lasting value. Given below are few ways of this learning process:

Motivation: Unless a person wants to learn there is little that the other members of the group or the trainer can do to help. However, we should remember that the desire to learn is likely to be present if other competing motives, *e.g.,* to protect ones self from threat, are reduced.

Diagnosis: We should continually gather data on the processes occurring in the group in order that we can be aware of what is happening.

Observation: If we are aware of what is happening, we can understand better why it is happening and what might improve the effectiveness of our group. Our idea of what we might do is a provisional hypothesis.

Action: We will never be able to know if our hypothesis is correct unless we are willing to test it in action. If the direction following our action is more appropriate then we may have confirmed our hypothesis. If not, then we may need to gather data on why it was not. Perhaps our diagnosis or our hypothesis was incorrect.

In T-Group we learn to identify some of the factors which are important in this process. Often people find it difficult what to talk in a T-Group. We can talk about our behaviour; we can discuss our impressions of it with others. Our impressions can be compared with others who have experienced certain aspects of our behaviour. Our behaviour can be talked about descriptively: We do not find it necessary to evaluate behaviour as good or bad but rather our perceptions of the behaviour and our feelings about it. Too often we try to place moralistic interpretations about the person on the basis of his behaviour. Clearly, such talk can be very difficult for the person to accept and it will provide little learning as a result.

This can be done in an atmosphere of reduced threat. In the training group we have an opportunity to find ways of supporting each other and of talking about our behavior in such a way that we gradually find less and less threat in our work. We can control our own learning and actions and ask for group's help in this process. We can say that I would like to try out a certain assumption or way of behaving and that I would like to get certain information (perceptions or reactions) from others to test this behaviour and in this way. This will help me to have control over my own learning.

Last, but perhaps most significant, we can adopt, experiment and try different attitude with respect to all of our behaviour. The norm of the group can be accepted that it is everyone's responsibility to deal with a certain issue confronting him or the group. This behaviour can be looked at, assessed. As the person experiments with different kinds of behaviour he can gradually develop greater flexibility in dealing with other people in different situations with different problems. It is this norm that we earlier referred to as the "right to be wrong." It is essential if we are to learn how to learn.

Conclusion: If we wish to learn more effective ways of working in groups we must begin the process by developing greater awareness of what is happening, we must try to understand this and try out ways of behaving which lead to more constructive action in our working relationships.

❑❑❑

Chapter 3

Dynamics of Silence in T-Group

> *"There are times when silence has the loudest voice."*
> **– Leroy Brownlow**

Moments of silence are integral part of T-Groups, especially in the early phases of a group's development. All the groups, I have worked with, almost every session started with silence. When silent members were queried on what they were thinking and feeling about events taking place in the group, they often replied, they had nothing to say as they did not feel anything. Later, as the group developed, these relatively silent members brought so much insights and depth of feelings to the group that not only other group members were astonished, but they themselves often discovered that, although they were silent, they had much to say, that was of value in understanding what was happening in the group and that they had a wide range of emotions about the events taking place in the group.

Emotions are important part of interpersonal relationships, whether or not we are aware of them or whether or not we choose to discuss them openly. Usually emotions are seen as potentially dangerous and destructive, thereby needing to be avoided and controlled carefully so that they do not surface in relationships. Emotions that arise in working together are not an illness; they are part of the human condition and tell us what matters most and what is really going on between us.

Everyone has various experiences, perceptions, thoughts, feeling, and emotional reactions while working in the group. Members of a group become angry with each other, they feel threatened, they become upset, they become defensive, they feel hurt, they feel sad, they feel disappointed, they feel affirmed, they feel elated, they feel passionate about something, they feel discouraged, they feel alone, they feel manipulated, they feel frustrated, they feel competitive, and they experience pain and a whole multitude of other emotions. Within the life of a group one can at one moment experience laughter and in another moment experience tears. Commitment, ownership, and passion are common emotions that occur in groups.

When people withhold their emotions and experiences in the group, for some reason, they believe that their inner experiences have no meaningful value for anyone and their contributions are meaningless. They do not share what they feel and think in the group because of the fear that any open expression of their emotions would indicate that they were in need of a psychotherapist. People, who do not share their experiences, not only deprive the group of valuable resource for learning, but also do not learn to deal with their own emotions or the emotions of others. When group members begin to acknowledge and express their emotions, they learn how to manage the emotional life of the group more creatively.

Various consequences of unexpressed emotions can be people suffer in silence, their feelings become distorted and go underground and seep out in the form of escalating fears, mistrust, gossip, rumors, scapegoating, apathy, boredom, feelings of stagnation, alienation, and a sense of being lonely in the midst of a group. People who have denied or blunted their feelings have not developed ways of expressing them. Feelings to them seem like a secret code or foreign language that is unknown and mysterious. With practice, however, they become more expressive and enjoy it. Expressiveness need not be simply verbal; learning to embrace people with a hug can be an awkward experience but, with practice, one develops a sense of spontaneity, stemming from what is happening in the relationship.

Interpersonal communication can be non-verbal does not need any language. For example, a smile: an angry tone of voice: a trembling lip: a cold stare: a defensive stance is all non-verbal ways to convey a message without translating it into language. There are usually several ways that we can express a particular experience in language. This means that we can explore several ways of expressing ourselves to discover impact and meaningful ways of elating to one another. Being open to exploring ways of expressing ourselves to one another is often an exciting and rich experience.

Coping with the expression of emotions by others can cause us to feel apprehensive and frightened. For example, if a group member feels hurt and begins to cry the other members can become apprehensive, partly because it stirs up their own hurts or sadness and partly because they are not sure how to respond. In fact, all they need to do is be with the person in a supportive way. They do not need to do anything to "fix" the person; the crying will end. At times a group uses one member to express emotions for the others. The important learning task for the group is to acknowledge their emotional pain and to learn how to express it personally.

Similarly, members of a group may be apprehensive about how to respond to an angry outburst. Chances are that the angry member is not alone in having the angry feelings. The learning task for the group is for the other members to acknowledge and express their angry feelings, rather than pretend that only one member is angry. Group members can support both the angry member and the member who becomes the target for the anger. When they are able to acknowledge and discuss their reaction openly, they discover that the expression of anger brings them closer together, that they can all handle it in a constructive way, and that they can learn from it in a meaningful way.

Sometimes the process is quite uncomfortable, awkward, confusing, and messy. It takes courage to learn. For members of a group to make the most of the opportunity, they must have intention to learn from one another in a constructive way. This may mean that, when heated exchanges take place, the members wait until things cool down so that they can examine what happened in a less impassioned way and heal whatever wounds occurred. The awkwardness and discomfort we feel in learning a new skill can be a relatively small cost for the benefits we can gain by developing our ability to acknowledge and express our experience. We can authorize ourselves to experience, express, and discuss our perceptions and emotions. With awareness and practice, we can become more complete in the way we create meaningfulness in our lives within groups.

Culture also plays an important role in the expression of emotions. Most of us live in a culture that discourages introspection and emotional closeness in relationships, particularly in the context of work. There are many explicit and hidden cultural messages that can discourage communication of our experiences and emotions. Messages such as "suffer in silence"; "don't cry"; "don't show that you're afraid"; "don't get angry"; "don't get too close"; and "don't upset others" discourage open expression of feelings. We are used to engaging in social rituals, roles, and pretense in each other's presence, rather than expressing our experiences more openly and deeply. Sometimes we receive such messages explicitly, and sometimes we infer them from observing the behaviour of others. No one has intentionally said this, but we assume that emotions are not discussed because there is something wrong with them or that it is dangerous to do so because things might get out of control. Most of us are fearful of our own emotions—of losing conscious control and being overpowered and controlled by them.

Any group must establish boundaries in regard to what emotions and experiences to express within the group and what emotions and experiences not to be shared within the group. The most important experiences and emotions to express are the immediate ones happening in group itself. The emotions, members hold about what is happening in the group and what is happening to them in *vis-à-vis* other group members are directly relevant to the work they are doing together. The past experiences that members bring with them to the group are not important for group working. Probably the most important experiences are the memories that are triggered by being in the group. For example, a member who angrily walks out of the group and slams the door may have memories of similar times when he or she had similar feelings. The strong expression of emotions by one member can also trigger the memories of other members, and it may be quite productive to discuss these memories with the purpose of understanding their implications for the development of the group.

❑❑❑

Chapter 4

"Are T-Group Experiences Applicable in Real World?"

> *"Never doubt that a small group of thoughtful, committed citizens can change the world; indeed, it's the only thing that ever has."*
>
> **–Margaret Mead**

The T-Group is over, participants are saying goodbye with tearful eyes and heavy hearts. Everyone is in the state of euphoria. They still carry the hangover of T-Group and feel as if they have come out of entirely different world. They wonder, "How will I apply what I have learned in real life?" Some of the experiences at T-Group are powerful, but are they applicable in real life also? This is the dilemma every participant faces.

A T-Group typically generates more feelings and interaction between participants than the groups to which they are accustomed to. For most participants "real worlds" might be a lecture class that is structured to limited communications between class teacher and students, a committee in which the group is organised so that all comments are addressed to the chair, or to departments that carefully avoid all but the most formal communication. The genuineness of the feelings generated by these structures is seldom questioned.

The question is, how does one generalise from the reality of the laboratory to the reality back home? There is no precise formula for answering this question, but there are two extreme positions to be avoided *i.e.,* overgeneralisation or under-generalisation. Both are not true and applicable in real life. The overgeneralisation is assumption that everything learned in a laboratory can be transplanted back home. It ignores the differences between the two worlds. There are long-term association and a whole variety of home and work relationships which must keep functioning in real life. One must keep that in mind while experimenting with new behaviour or expressing newly discovered feelings.

Under-generalisation involves assuming that the feelings, reactions, and processes discovered in the workshop can exist only in that special atmosphere. This also is not true. The structure of groups, for example, has an equal impact in and out of the T-Group. Using a flipchart involves people in a group's work whether that is a T-Group, a classroom or conference room).

In laboratory education participants typically experience new grouping and structures which generate new or relatively unfamiliar feelings. As an example of how a simple change in structure generates new feelings, consider the sitting arrangement (mattresses on the floor for every one, including the facilitator), made in T-Groups or addressing everyone one by first names communicate that everyone is equal in the group and thus influences the feelings of participants.

Another example is use of flipcharts in T-Groups for brain-storming, decision making, summarising of ideas, etc. That brings about changes in the structure and process of a group and thus influences the feelings of participants. When a group uses a flipchart, every member has equal access to the accumulation of ideas contrary to "real" situation in which one individual writes down ideas or an agenda on a single sheet of paper visible only to that person. In using a flipchart every group member has the information to state whether a particular option has already been listed, phrased correctly, coded appropriately, etc. The reality of a laboratory experience hinges upon the reality of the feelings engendered and experienced there. The special structures and the limited duration of the laboratory group encourage individuals to experience a new range of feelings.

These "new" feelings are discovered, not created; that is to say, rarely are they, in fact, new. For example, a participant who is interrupted or criticised back home in the "real world" may feel embarrassment rather than anger or hurt. Embarrassment for this person is thus a substitute feeling. For another the substitute may be guilt (or frustration or impatience). More basic feelings, such as hurt and anger, may be "discovered" at T-Group. The fact is that these basic feelings are "real" and so are the laboratory experiences which helped someone to discover them.

Another less-than-real aspect of laboratory education for some people is the temporary nature of most group associations. "How can this be real if I probably will never see these people again"? If the criterion for "realness" is long-term association, workshops and laboratories are not real. If, however, the criterion is the internal awareness of authentic feelings of genuine reactions to others; then laboratory experience is very real indeed. For example, the individual who discovers that beneath the surface of embarrassment is a more basic feeling of fear may also realise that it has been around for a long time. This recognition, then, is a re-introduction to a piece of individual reality that for a while had not been available. The only difference is that at the back-home situation embarrassment was substituted for fear, whereas in the laboratory situation fear is acknowledged.

To conclude, feelings can have a similar impact upon behaviour in both situations, a T-Group as well as back-home situations. The reality of Laboratory experience thus lies not in the permanence or structure of the group but rather in the feelings and the human experience common to all situations. Learnings from T-Group can be transferred to back-home situations with sensitivity to others and the situation.

❐❐❐

Chapter 5

How to Write a Personal Journal?

> *Personal diary or journal is like having a place to collect your thoughts and feelings in a more definite way. Writing things down forces you to be deeper and more precise.*
>
> **–Anonymous**

Journal writing or maintaining logs is one of the crucial ingredients or part of learning in a T-Group. It, not only is crucial learning in a laboratory setting, but also in every day life. Each of us experience life in a unique way and that is worth writing about! The purpose of the journal is to keep record of the major events in your life. When we talk about major, we do not mean only once a year or once in a couple of year. We mean that you need to write the journal everyday and capture the important moments in your life. Why is it so important? It is because writing on the journal will give you the opportunity to review what you have done. Also it will let you evaluate your feeling at the moment and find out what you can do differently if the result does not come out the way you want.

We can increase our competence to know, value, and choose our life path by a variety of methods. Writing down our life flow in a systematic way and using it as a guide is one method to know ourselves better, to see and hear ourselves in new ways and to be able to incorporate this information into our next experiences. Writing a journal can also let you absorb details of the event that you may forget after time goes by. You will be able to capture moment of joy and sadness. You can get into that moment every time you want to by reading and reviewing it. We remember that success happens in the mind. And this is the best way to practice our mind about how to feel by using our own history records as a guideline.

Perhaps one of the most difficult learning tasks we have is working with ourselves and that is purpose of T-Group; *i.e.* self-awareness. The T-Group setting is often a good place to start a new process, behaviour, or technique, but it then must be built into one's daily repertoire back home, at work, with family, and/or with other shared relationships. Effective journal keeping can be a means for deepening our insights into the total flow of our life processes, learning to perceive and attend to the self in new ways, discovering new dimensions of the self, and developing a personal feedback system. The personal journal is one such process technique.

Personal journal offers an opportunity for engaging one-self in experience and something we can transfer with relative ease from laboratory to back-home. Be specific about your day, your thoughts and feelings. Name the people you are with, even if you have a code for them in your journal. Name the place you are sitting to eat your meal or sip your coffee. When it comes to thoughts and emotions try your best to describe how you are feeling. If you recognise the emotion then name it. If you cannot find the correct name for what you are going through then do your best to describe it. You might need to lean towards metaphor to help you out, but try not to use clichés and tired sayings. Lend a fresh voice to your entries by trying to use descriptions from what you know and understand.

Some of the reasons, why writing a journal is important and integral part of your laboratory experience are:

- **To experiment with new behaviour:** If you have never kept a personal journal this may well be a new behaviour.
- **To develop an internal feedback system for you :** It feeds back to you what, how and where you were during the course of a day. It is different form feedback requested and received from others. It is indeed an internal dialogue.

- **To express feelings freely and to explore those feeling moments:** Reflect on the person, tasks, processes and specific stimuli that evoke emotional responses in you and on your own behaviour with those feelings and persons. Through this expressive/reflective process we learn what our own dynamics are-our own energising patterns.

- **To learn more about important aspects of our lives:**

  (a) Our personal history – "Where have I been in my life?"

  (b) Our current status – "What brings me to this 'now' place and what do I perceive about myself in relation to this space/time reality?"

  (c) Our future potential – "Where am I going?" "Who is this person moving into the future?"

- **To enhance our capacity to be aware of the inner dynamics or movement of our own loves:** It can help to expand our consciousness of the body-mind-spirit unity of ourselves, to increase our sensitivity to ourselves and to respond with similar sensitivity to others. As we dig our own personal well, we may eventually reach the underground river from which our basic unity springs.

Your laboratory experiences and your journal are steps towards freedom and responsibility. Your journal can become the vehicle through which you discover you own way in the world. The most effective work with the journal occurs when you set aside some times each day for writing, at least a half hour daily during your laboratory. Developing this discipline back home can be difficult.

One technique you can use when writing in your journal is to make sure you note down thc details. You will find the missing details are the most frustrating part about rereading your journal entries. Make an effort to write specific details in your journal. Three things need to be answered before you start writing your journal. *Firstly,* what should be written about, *secondly,* what to write and finally what would be the benefit.

1. Events

What to write?: What happened in sequence? How did the events start? How did it end? When in time did it start? End? List the people, things, content of the event.

What would be the benefit?: Increased awareness of timing cues you use to know when something begins and ends; Increased skills in describing behavioural sequence in an interaction process.

2. People

What to write?: Name persons, describe them physically: sex, race, age, height, weight, physical condition. Note the ones who were most important to you. Describe their behaviour, verbal and/or non-verbal, which made an impact on you.

What would be the benefit?: Increased observation skills, increased ability to identify what types of persons and/or behaviours evoke a response in you. Increased awareness of what you attend to and do not attend to with other persons.

3. Feelings

What to write?: What you felt/feel? How your body felt/feels (was there a change in breathing? What non-verbal, physical cues were present at the time the feeling was recognised?) What was the flow of feeling during the day – the highs, the lows, the neutral or quiet times? Who or what when the feelings occurred?

What would be the benefit?: Increased awareness of your learning, synthesis of your daily life experiences, sensitivity to your own wisdom, potential sources for action in the laboratory or back home.

4. Striking thoughts of "insights"

What to write?: Write out the complete thought. If possible, describe what you were doing when the thought occurred. Write down any other associations you make with the thought. Make a full report.

What would be the benefit?: Increased awareness of your learning, synthesis of your daily life experience, sensitivity to your own wisdom, potential sources for action in the laboratory or back home.

5. Experiences with ideas

What to write?: Ideas may come from yourself, other people or books. Write them down briefly (2 or 3 sentences). Describe their impact on you.

What would be the benefit?: Increased awareness of extent to which ideas, language and thought affect you and have impact on your behaviour.

6. Experiences with things

What to write?: Paintings, plays water, novels, books, trees, flowers, food and rocks are only a few of the things which may impact you during a day. Note them.

What would be the benefit?: Recognition and appreciation of non-human materials and your sensitivity to them.

7. Dreams/ Fantasies

What to write?: Write out the dream completely and accurately, with as much details as possible.

What would be the benefit?: Knowledge about your own personal symbolic language, a new means of your understanding your life experiences from an inner perspective.

These suggestions may help you build in this personal time back home.

1. Review your current weekly schedule. Identify the time you spend alone now. If none, then review your schedule a second time and look for possible times when you could be alone.
2. Set a realistic goal for writing in your journal. This may begin with once a week twice or three times each week.
3. Do not punish yourself with negative thoughts and evaluations if you do not adhere to your schedule immediately.
4. Begin writing those parts of the journal that are easy for you, then move to the less familiar and more difficult parts.
5. Determine to have some alone time on a regular basis for yourself, and then remember to do it.

❑❑❑

Part Two

Individual & Group Processes

Chapter 6

Significance of Observations in a Group

> *"The power of accurate observation is commonly called cynicism by those who haven't got it."*
> **–George Bernard Shaw**

Observation is the most important and an integral part of learning in a group. The only way to learn self, others and group processes is to observe and analyze what is happening in one's T-Group. All of us have spent our lives in groups of various sorts like, family, friends, team, workgroup, school, college and so on – but rarely have we taken the time to observe, discuss, and try to understand what was going on in the group. T-Group provides an excellent opportunity and a safe place to practice the skill of observation. One of the main goals of T-Group is to become better observers, which may help a person to become more effective group participants, also.

One way of gathering data about groups in order to understand their behaviour better is thorough observation. To become more sensitive observers we need to pay attention to two questions. (1) What do we look for within the complexities of group behaviour which will help us to understand what is going on in the group? (2) How do I function as an observer of group behaviour?

What to Look for in a Group?

1. **Physical structure or arrangement:** How are people arranged in the group in geographical relation to one another–in a circle, on the floor, around a table or in rows? These and other arrangements affect how people participate with each other. Usually fuller communication occurs when people can see as well as hear each other.

2. **Formal and informal structure:** Often in groups some members have been formally assigned positions and functions such as chairman, secretary, facilitator, teacher, etc. Their positions affect how these people behave in the group as well as how other people behave towards them. Informal structures also develop in groups - people who are friends or know each other well may form cliques. Their liking each other probably makes them to communicate more easily with each other than with others in the group.

3. **Participation:** Participation is the most important aspect to observe. Some of the indicators are: (a) frequency and (b) pattern of participation. An observer may observe who is talking and who is not talking. This gives accurate information about members who have participated overtly and those who have not. It does not give any indication of silent participation by members who have talked little or not at all. Each member in a group follows some patterns; *e.g.*, some talk to some specific people or some member may always talk immediately after particular member of the group or to the designated loader. These patterns may be observed and plotted. Such patterns sometimes give clues to cliques and factions in a group, power relations in a group, etc.

4. **Member contributions:** One may observe not just the frequency or pattern of member participation, but also try to identify the function and purpose of contributions made. One way of observing a problem solving group in this way is to distinguish between two general kinds of member participation: (a) task contributions *e.g.*, initiating ideas or perceptions, giving information, seeking information, giving

ideas or perception, giving opinion, seeking opinion, clarifying, summarising, testing consensus, *etc.,* and *(b)* building and maintenance contributions, *e.g.* encouraging, harmonising, standard setting, making observations about how the group is getting along, relieving tension, etc.

5. **Group goals:** An observer may watch a group to see in what direction it is moving from time to time. Some goal directives may be clear, others not so clear. It may be useful to watch for both stated (overt) goals and unstated (implicit) goals. Most groups have both an open agenda and a hidden agenda. Learning to open up and understand hidden agenda may help to improve both the quality of participation by members and the productivity of the group as a whole.
6. **Group standards:** Every group develops or takes over from other associations certain norms with respect to what is expected by way of behaviour from all members and from special members. There are some things we do not talk about, other things that are within bounds. All members may be expected to participate equally or some members are expected to contribute more than others. Members may be expected to assemble on time or the norm may be getting there 5 or 10 minutes after the stated time. Norms or standards may be explicit or implicit. The group tends to reward members who conform to the norms and punish those who deviate from them.
7. **Group atmosphere:** There is a vague term which attempts to describe the general emotional tones of a group. We may observe that the atmosphere is tense or relaxed, friendly or hostile, polite or impolite, etc. of course, the atmosphere may change from time and the thoughtful observer will try to figure out why this is so.

To summarise an observer has to follow three different processes when observing a group:

(1) Observation, *e.g.,* what is actually going on?

(2) Analysis; *e.g.,* what do my observations mean – in terms of the past listing of the group, its present conditions and problems and its future?

(3) Evaluation; *e.g.*, to evaluate what set of values or criteria are used. Evaluation involves a judgment about whether the condition of the group is good or bad, right or wrong, etc.

A frequent temptation of observers is that they let their values colour their observations and analyze in such a way that they have difficulty in seeing what is actually happening and what it probably means. To conclude various things, which can be observed in a group are *content and process, communication process, decision-making procedures, self-oriented vs. concern for group task behaviour, various emotional issues and ways of dealing with them, etc.*

1. Content and Process

Any group operates at two levels simultaneously, with events occurring at both "content" and "process" levels. The content of a group's activity is the tip of the iceberg and includes visible or apparent occurrences. When we observe what the group is talking about, we are focusing on the content. As with an iceberg, substantial group interaction occurs below the water line. Group process is less apparent than content but no less important in achieving group goals.

Process relates "how we do it," including group members' personal needs, informal leadership, norms, feelings, and hidden agendas. Effective groups lower the water line as much as possible, so that content and process are treated equally. When we try to observe how the group is handling its communication *e.g.,* who talks how much or who talks to whom, we are focusing on group process. An observer should pay attention to critical process issues: decision-making methods, quality of communication, roles group members may play etc..

Most discussion topics about the back-home situation emphasise the content: "What is good leadership?" "How can I motivate my subordinate?" "How can we make meetings more effective?" They concern issues which are "there and then" in the sense of being abstract, future or past oriented and not involving group members directly. In focusing on group process, we are looking at what the group is doing in the "here and now" it is working in the sense of its present behaviours.

In fact, the content of the conversation is often the best clue as to what process issue may be on people's minds when they find it difficult to confront the issue directly. For example, when group talks about problem of authority back home may mean that there is a leadership struggle going on in the T-Group; talking about people back home in office, who do not really help anybody may mean dissatisfaction with the way the trainer in the T-Group is behaving; talking about how bad group meetings usually are in the office may mean that members are dissatisfied with the way meetings of their own T-Group are going on. At a simpler level, looking at process really means to focus on what is going on in the group explicitly and try to understand it in terms of other things that are happening implicitly in the group.

2. Communication

A group process observer must develop an ability to recognise key characteristics of a group's communication, including direction, openness, non-verbal communication etc. The kind of observations made give clues to other important things which may be going on in the group, such as who leads whom or who influences whom. Things that can be observed are:

- ❑ Does everyone feel free to communicate with all other members? Is communication centered on the trainer?
- ❑ Do individuals feel free to express their feelings?
- ❑ What is the tone of group feelings: enthusiasm, belligerence, boredom, or acceptance?
- ❑ Is everyone making an effort to listen and understand before responding?
- ❑ Who talks, for how long and how often?
- ❑ Whom do people look at when they talk? Whole group, some favourite persons, or ceiling or floor.
- ❑ Who supports whom; the group as a whole, the trainer, any specific member or no one?

- Who talks after whom? Who interrupts whom?
- What style of communication is used assertive, aggressive, submissive, questioning, supportive or not supportive, humorous, finicky etc.? Tone of voice and gestures should also be observed.
- Are all members participating or some members are quite?

Easiest way to observe all about thing much more is, the observer should note down the names of all group members and plot a mark, next to the name he or she speaks. Observer can also note down the duration each member speaks. It has been seen that many silent members are accused of not speaking, but they say they spoke, but no one listened to them. In fact data can show they were speaking, but they were stereotyped by the group as silent members and were actually not listened to. An observer can help the group to look at all these issues.

3. Decision Making Procedures

Performance of a group involves taking into account the needs and opinions of every group member, being able to come to an equitable decision as efficiently as possible are important for the functioning of the group. Whether we are aware of it or not groups are making decisions all the time, some of them without much awareness and in reference to group procedures or standards of operation. It is important to observe how decisions are made in a group in order to assess the appropriateness of the method to the matter being decided on and in order to access whether the consequences of given method are really what the group members bargained for.

Group decisions are notoriously hard to undo. When someone says, "Well, we decided to do it, didn't we?" any budding opposition is quickly immobilised. Often we can undo the decision only if we reconstruct it, understand how we made it and test was appropriate or not. Some methods by which groups make decisions are as following:

Decision by lack of response (The Plop): "I think we should introduce ourselves"... silence.

The self-authorized agenda (Decision by one): I think we should introduce ourselves; my name is Joe Smith…

Decision by a minority-one or more: "Does Anyone Object or "We all agree,"

Decision by majority (Majority – Minority Voting Polling): "Let us see where everyone stands; what do you think?"

Consensus testing: Exploration to set for opposition and to determine whether opposition feels strongly enough to be unwilling to implement decision: not necessarily unanimity but essential agreement by all.

The process of decision-making can be tricky. For example, it sometimes happens that a decision to poll-which looks very democratic, because polling is considered democratic – can be made by self-authorization or by handclasp. At such a point, the alert group members will realise what is going on and insist that the group be clear on its decision-making style. Actually, the decision a group makes about how it will make decisions can be the most important single element with respect to how it works as a group.

4. Task or Maintenance Functions

Group members tend to take several roles within a group. These roles fall under broad categories:

- Task roles involve getting the job done no matter what,
- Initiators contribute new ideas or encourage new directions,
- Summarisers pull things together, recap, or add perspective,
- Clarifiers help others understand what is occurring,
- Information seekers ask for input or direction.

Behaviour in the group can be seen from the point of view of what its purpose or function seems to be. When a member says something, is he primarily trying to get the group task accomplished (task)., or to meet some personal need or goal without regard to the group's problems (self-oriented).

A. The types of behaviour relevant to the group's fulfillment of its task are these:

- **Initiating:** Proposing tasks or goals: defining a group problem; suggesting a procedure or ideas for solving problem…
- **Seeking information or opinions:** Requesting facts; seeking relevant information about concern; requesting statements or estimate; soliciting expressions of value; seeking suggestions and ideas…
- **Giving infirmation or opinions:** Offering facts, providing relevant information about group concern; stating a belief about a matter before the group;…
- **Summarising:** Pulling together related idea; resulting suggestions after the group has discussed them; offering a decision or conclusion for the group to accept or reject.
- **Consensus testing:** Asking to see whether the group is nearing a decision, sending up a trial balloon to test a possible…

B. Types of behaviours relevant to the group's remaining in good working order, having a good climate for task work, and good relationships which permit maximum use of member resources, *i.e.,* group maintenance, are as follows:

- **Harmonising:** Attempting to reconcile disagreement; reducing tension; getting people to explore differences…
- **Gate keeping:** Helping to keep communication channels open; facilitating the participation of others; suggesting procedures that permit sharing remarks…
- **Encouraging:** Being friendly, warm and responsive to others; indicating by facial expression or remarks the acceptance of others' contributions…
- **Compromising:** When own idea or status is involved in a conflict, offering a compromise which yields status; admitting error; modifying in interest of group cohesion or growth…

- **Standard setting and testing:** Testing whether the group is satisfied with its procedures or suggesting procedures; pointing out explicit or implicit norms which have been set to make them available for testing…

Every group needs both kinds of behaviour and needs to work out an adequate balance of tasks and maintenance activities.

5. Emotional Issues : Causes of Self-oriented, Emotional Behaviour

The processes described so far deal with the group's attempts to work, to solve problems of tasks and maintenance; but there are many forces active in groups which disturb work, which represent a kind of emotional underworld undercurrent in the stream of group life. The underlying emotional issues produce a variety of behaviours which interfere with or are destructive of effective group functioning. Group often ignores such an issue or wishes it away, an action that can be detrimental to their task accomplishment as well as to the growth of the individual(s) whose behaviour is based on self-oriented needs. The effective group will recognise what is going on, try to identify the issue, and then work with it in ways which permit these same emotional energies to be channeled in the direction of the group's effort.

A. What are these emotional issues or basic problems?

- **Identity:** Who am I in this group? Where do I fit in? What kind of behaviour is acceptable here?
- **Goal and needs:** What do I want from the group? Can the group goals be made consistent with my goals? What have I to offer to the group?
- **Power, control and influence:** Who will control what? How much power and influence do I have?
- **Intimacy:** How close will we get to each other? How personal? How much can we trust each other? Can we achieve a greater trust?

B. What kinds of behaviours are produced in response to these problems?

- **Dependency- counter dependency:** Opposing or resisting anyone in the group who represents authority.
- **Fighting and controlling:** Asserting personal dominance, attempting to get own way regardless of others.
- **Withdrawing:** Trying to remove the sources of uncomfortable feelings by psychologically leaving the group.
- **Pairing up:** Seeking out one or two supporters and forming a kind of emotional subgroup in which members protect and support one another.

These are not the only phenomenon which can be observed in the group. What is important to observe will vary with what the group is doing, the needs and purposes of the observer, and many other factors. The main point, however, is that improving our skills in observing what is going on in the group will provide us with important data for understanding groups and increasing our effectiveness within them. Often, the most effective and useful group member will be the one who can function as "participant/ observer", contributing to the group's task accomplishment, yet still able to use a "third eye" to observe how the group is working – information which he shares with the group at appropriate times in an effort to help it deal with the group at appropriate times in an effort to help it deal with maintenance issues and blockages arising out of self-oriented needs.

❒❒❒

Chapter 7

Various Group Processes

> *"Conflict is inevitable in a team ... in fact, to achieve synergistic solutions, a variety of ideas and approaches are needed. These are the ingredients for conflict."*
>
> **–Susan Gerke,**
> **IBM, Leadership Development**

Various processes take place in the life of a group. These processes can be either beneficial or detrimental to the welfare of group members. The five major growth processes that can be observed in groups are self-awareness, self-disclosure, feedback, risk taking, and consensual validation. Interaction of these processes accounts for shaping the behaviour of individuals. Understanding these processes is important in order to make "wise" choices, based on three criteria: awareness of self, awareness of options, and willingness to take responsibility for consequences. These processes are directly related to the various stages of group development.

Learning groups provide data to individuals and give them a space where they can try new ways of behaving. Above mentioned processes are the principal vehicles for change, and these processes should be initiated deliberately. The facilitator can help to promote trust by modelling and encouraging others to engage in self-awareness, self-disclosure, feedback, trust and risk taking, etc.

1. Self – Awareness

The aim of the T-Group is to help a person to grow in self-awareness as a precondition to making wise choices. The composition of the group is important. If there is too much homogeneity, the individual may not learn how other kinds of people may react to him or her. Conversely, if the group is too heterogeneous, some individuals may experience anxiety about being "different" and may not participate fully. A good guideline is one of controlled variety: maximum difference with the condition that no person feels unable to identify with any other member.

The core of personal learning is looking clearly at oneself. Unfortunately, our ability to distort information about ourselves is almost limitless. The key to individual growth in any effort that can be described as humanistic is self-assessment. The first criterion of the "wise" choice is self-awareness. As you grow in self-awareness, you will better understand why you feel what you feel and why you behave as you behave. That understanding then gives you the opportunity and freedom to change those things you would like to change about yourself and create the life you want. Without fully knowing who you are, self-acceptance and change become impossible.

The concept that an individual has about self is a remarkably stable aspect of personality. It has a profound effect on how the person behaves or chooses not to behave. Our self-concepts come from "significant others", usually in the formative years. Sometimes, what we learnt about ourselves from those whom we have trusted, shapes large parts of our lives. We all have self-concepts, although we may not be aware of what they are. We defend ourselves when we feel threatened and we open ourselves to learning in a high-trust situation. It is as though the self-concept is surrounded by a membrane that is thick under threat and permeable with trust.

In any group in which members are looking critically at themselves, there is the likelihood that new insights will emerge. If the group exists to promote growth in the part of its members, it needs to emphasise the need to relate what happens in the group to individuals. They key questions often are: "Who am I?" "What am I up to?", "Where am I going?", and "What difference does it make anyway?" In order for group members to be able to see themselves more clearly, additional processes must be followed. Interacting with others can provide new data about oneself.

2. Self-Disclosure

Self-disclosure is seen as a useful strategy for sharing information with others. By sharing information, we become more intimate with other people and our interpersonal relationship is strengthened the concept. Self-disclosure is not simply providing information to another person. Instead, scholars define self-disclosure as sharing information with others that they would not normally know or discover. Self-disclosure involves risk and vulnerability on the part of the person sharing the information.

It's important to know that self-disclosure does not involve "dumping" everything about yourself on everyone from close friends to complete strangers. Obviously self-disclosure needs to happen in context, be appropriate for the particular relationships. While self-disclosure is important, remember that communication means sharing of information from both sides, and if you are inundating the other person with too much information about yourself, or information they really have no interest in, then the whole thing is going to backfire, because you will appear selfish and self-centered.

Talking about oneself in a group setting is just one form of disclosure and is a potentially useful way of discovering patterns. Sharing feelings with others can be both cathartic and enlightening. We mediate our self-disclosure by choosing what to reveal, in accordance with our perceptions of what is appropriate in the situation. Group norms can have a significant effect in this. We hold back less in an atmosphere of trust than we do when we feel threatened.

3. Feedback

Feedback refers to the sharing of interpersonal perceptions and reactions. We give feedback by telling others how their behaviour affects us. This process greatly affects our self-concepts, when feedback is from someone whom one mistrusts. In a group situation, there is potential for both constructive and destructive feedback. Feedback process is so powerful - especially when it is requested – it can result in a narrowing of one's choices as well as clearer understanding of oneself.

There are some generally accepted guidelines about what constitutes useful interpersonal feedback in groups. One thing to keep in mind is that the feedback should be clear so that it can be easily understood by the group member receiving it. Keeping the feedback concise and direct will help make it clear. Another quality feedback should have is that it should be relevant. Relevant feedback is often directed to something that is happening in the group at that moment and will tend to elicit a response or reaction from the person receiving it. An aspect of feedback that is often overlooked is that effective feedback will focus on the sender. This usually makes it easier for the person receiving feedback to really listen and take it in. Useful feedback also tends to include emotions, involve some self-disclosure, and will avoid being judgmental. Lastly, one hallmark of successful interpersonal feedback is that it will say something about the relationship between the sender and the receiver.

Feedback needs to be managed well. When an individual solicits concrete, descriptive statements from others about the effects of that individual's behaviour, that person's self-concept is probably the most permeable. If the feedback is targeted toward the growth goals of the individual, the data are likely to be useful. However, the process is risky.

Feedback that is received from many people is more powerful than feedback that is received from one person. One develops the idea that one is loveable (or stupid, or competent) by hearing that message from more than one person whom one trusts. This does not, by the way, mean that the feedback is accurate, but the consensus "validates" the information and increases the chances that one will internalise the characterisation. Validation of feedback is one of the most powerful processes that occur in groups. It can serve as a mechanism for "correcting" one's self-concept, for counteracting one's tendency to practice self-deception.

4. Trust and Risk-Taking

Participants share a certain degree of personal risk sending messages and providing feedback to one another. If members of the group do not trust other members, they will be less willing to participate and express ideas. For example, if an individual is constantly attacked, put down or told that they are wrong, that person will be less likely to continue to participate. When members feel that they do not trust one another, they will withhold the vital feedback necessary for all members to achieve understanding, higher task performance and greater productivity.

As a measure of trust, members of a team are constantly asking and answering the question: "If I were to openly express myself, will what I say be used against me." A member of a learning group will not test out hypotheses about new strategies or attempt to check out what has been understood, if another member is waiting for others to make a (mistake) so that he/she can correct. Trust and open participation would quickly deteriorate if this were to occur among the participants of a group.

Johnson and Johnson view the development of trust through a mutual exchange of trusting and trustworthy messages. "Trusting" behaviour is defined as openly expressing thoughts, feelings, reactions, information, ideas and resources. "Trustworthy" behaviour is defined as expressions of acceptance and high regard for the participants, expressions of support for the capabilities of members, and expressions that you are going to work with the other members of the group to achieve the group goals. Trusting and trustworthy behaviours will build upon each other to increase the level of participation and commitment to the learning goals of the group. Without conscious attention to the development and maintenance of trust in a group, the learning goals of the members will not be achieved or the group at best will on lower level learning or information exchange.

Some areas of the self are not directly accessible through reflection or discussion. One must take risks to reach them. Trying new ways of behaving can help us to discover parts of ourselves that we may have been afraid to explore and that may disconfirm certain aspects of our self-concepts. Obviously, some risks are foolish (the probability of negative out-comes is too high) and others have little growth potential (failure is unlikely). Trying out new behaviour in a group cannot only expand one's response repertoire, but also can disclose new parts of oneself.

If the group has high mutual trust, members are likely to receive support for experimenting with behaviour, especially if they announce what they are doing. This is one of the keys to building trust. Talking about trust does not instill confidence; that comes from working together on commonly agreed-on objective. The experience of success and of validated expectations of one another creates a feeling of safety.

❑❑❑

Chapter 8

Group Norms

> *"Coming together is a beginning, Keeping together is progress, Working together is success."*
>
> **–Henry Ford**

All groups have expressed and/or unexpressed norms of behaviour, or ways of doing things. These usually unspoken and unexamined "rules" determine what is acceptable and what is not acceptable behaviour in the group. Expressed norms may be in the form of written rules or procedures. Unexpressed norms may be understandings about the way in which members interrelate, how long meetings will last, how much frivolity will be included in meetings, and so on. Faculty meetings, for example, may have a rule that meetings will start at 11.00 a.m. and anybody watching the group, however, will note that the meetings usually start between 11.10 a.m. and 11.20 a.m. without anyone's taking exception to it. A new member of the group, who comes initially at 11.00 a.m., somehow learns this norm and starts coming between 11.10 a.m. and 11.20 a.m..

Norms are not good or bad; they are effective or ineffective; they help the group or they hinder it. Often we are not consciously aware of them but most of us must know they exist because we behave in ways that are responsive to them. Identifying and examining them is often hard work and we may struggle against it, but sometimes – especially when nothing seems to be going right, we keep wondering "what is O.K. to do in here and what is not O.K. to do." Often participants look initially to the trainer for such rules. In a T-Group, dealing with the here-and-now deprives group members of the false support of back-home status.

Over a period of time, as a group forms, for example, a T-Group, the group members somehow come to know that it is acceptable to do certain things, while some behaviors are not accepted. Since this usually happens without the group's conscious awareness, unstated norms can develop which block or hinder the group from doing what it really wants to do. For this reason it is often useful for a group to identify important norms, judge whether they are facilitating or blocking, and then decide how to go about developing new ones if the old will not do.

Norms can be facilitating or hindering. Collaborative behaviour places people in a relationship in which the important question is not "Who was right?" or "Who won't?" but "What can we or did we learn?" This reduces threat and encourages more for presentation of self, whereas competitiveness increases the risk of creating situations of win-lose, right-wrong, attack-defense etc. Some of the facilitating norms in T-Groups are Openness, risk-taking, self-disclosure, helpful feedback, experimentation etc. They are all necessary to the learning process of a T-Group.

Exhibit 8.1 : Some Group Norms

Facilitating Norms	***Hindering or Blocking Norms***
Collaborative behaviour	Competitive behaviour
Dealing with the here-and-now	Dealing with the there-and-then
Acceptance of my own and other's feelings;	Censoring and/or denying own and criticising or evaluating others' feelings.
Respect for the individual	Insistence upon conformity to the group
Describing other persons' behaviour	Inferring the motivation behind person's behaviour.
Recognition that behaviour has consequences.	Insistence that a person "should" or "should not" behave in a particular way.

Acceptance of own feelings and others' feelings is important to encourage group members to take risk of exposing themselves to others. Criticising or denying the feelings of others would block members to expose their feelings in the group, for example, if someone says, "You should not be angry" or "You are not really as angry as you say you are"? Will such responses increase willingness of members to share their feeling?

If the individual can be helped to see that a specific behaviour has specific consequences, rather than being told. "You should not do that!" he is free to decide for himself whether he is willing to accept those consequences instead. For example, if you tell me that when I interrupt you it makes you angry and therefore less likely to listen to what I am saying. I am than free to decide (among other alternatives) whether I want to stop interrupting you because I do not want you not to listen or whether I will continue interrupting you because that behavior is more important to me than is its impact on you.

A T-Group can create such an atmosphere; but it does not happen automatically simply because the members wish for it or because rules can be set and enforced. What is important is that in such a group openness is not likely to be increased by insistence on it (Is pressure likely to make you more open?). But the group may move towards greater openness by trying to find answers to the question. "What are we really doing with respect to openness, and what conditions exist here which bring about such behaviour?" Some of the facilitating norms in T-Groups are as follows:

1. Feedback

Individuals learn through developing behavioural patterns guided by clear and accurate feedback about the effectiveness and appropriateness of their actions. Feedback can come from a variety of sources; including other group members, group facilitators, observers, etc. Feedback must be based on valid data and should be relevant to behaviour and situations that can be changed or modified. The following is a summary of the general guidelines for giving feedback:

- Feedback should be specific and objective: it should describe observable behaviours, and words should be quoted directly.
- It should not be evaluative, make inferences, or attribute feelings or motives.
- It should be given only for behaviours that can be changed.
- It should describe the impact of the behaviour on the person who is giving the feedback.
- It should be requested by the recipient.

Accuracy of feedback can be checked or validated in the group setting. Group members receiving the feedback can be asked to state in their own words what they heard. The group also should provide support to the person receiving the feedback.Its purpose is to help the person to solve problems not to create new ones. The facilitator and group members can help in this process by suggesting alternative or new behaviors and by reinforcing positive attempts to changes.

2. Supportive Climate

A climate of trust and non-defensiveness is necessary for people to be able to take risk to share their ideas and feelings. All group members must have trust in the group to be able to take a risk to practice openness by giving and receiving feedback, right or wrong, effective or ineffective, without feeling that they are risking their membership in the group and acceptance of others. This does not mean that conflict, anger, or differences should be avoided. Indeed, such emotions are more acceptable in a supportive climate.

3. Experimentation

An important possibility in many group situations, especially in a T-Group, is the trying out alternative patterns of behaviour. With a supportive climate and with valid feedback, experimentation can be a key element in changing behaviour. Some people may, however, use experimentation defensively: "I did not really feel like that; I just did that to see what you would do. "The difference between useful and useless experimentation is that useful experimentation concerns one's *personal behaviour; whereas* experimenting with the behaviour of others is "playing games".

4. Goal Clarity

It is helpful when group members and facilitators have some clear goals and purpose. This is especially true in a T-Group. A lack of clear learning goals produces two problems: *firstly,* differences in individual learning needs cannot be handled, and *secondly,* it becomes difficult to determine the extent of progress. Goals are more helpful if they are related to specific behaviours and actions and checked against feedback. Although clear goals cannot be expected immediately, goal clarification and review should be a continuing process for individuals and for the group.

5. Communication

Usually only a small proportion of what is said in a group is heard or understood by many of the members. When someone talks, others might be thinking about what they would like to say next or would not say, they might be thinking, whatever the speaker really is saying is useless etc. Any of these distractions reduce the probability of listening. Observation of non-verbal communication activities is useful in this process.

Another issue that often arises in groups is when no one speaks or visibly participates in some way. If the facilitator does not generate a discussion or activity at that point, group members are likely to complain that "nothing is happening". The facilitator can take this opportunity to help the members to see what is happening, *i.e.,* to discuss the lack of communication at that point and what might be happening to cause it.

6. Group Growth and Maintenance

A group has development needs beyond the collective needs of its members; it needs time and assistance to become mature, effective, and cohesive. The need for group maintenance is closely related to group growth. In many group-learning models, members can use group maintenance to develop their skills in group diagnosis and group facilitation. Energy invested in group building and maintenance as a preventive rather than repair measure is a positive indicator of group health and growth. A facilitator can aid in this process by teaching the members about the roles of members in groups and by helping them to learn to identify and deal with dysfunctional behaviours.

7. Structure and Procedure

All groups have norms and procedures, and even disorder is a structure. It is not always sufficiently clear how formal the structure should be and whether it is imposed externally or derived internally. Structures are related to assumptions and values, as well as to the participants' abilities to cope with ambiguity. When a group can establish and maintain the degree of structure it needs for effective work and can change the structure as its needs and issues change, group growth is evident.

❑❑❑

Chapter 9

Stages of Group Development

> *"TEAM –Together Everyone Achieves More."*
> **–Anonymous**

Groups have been studied for years, and it has been discovered that new ones go through various stages as they develop toward highly functioning teams. Some groups move easily through these stages, but others may get seriously stuck, unable to move forward. Bruce Tuckman has provided us with what has become the staple of group dynamics, "Five Stages of Group Development." He first described the four stages of group development in 1965— forming, storming, norming, and performing and later, he added adjourning.

Looking at the behaviour of small groups in a variety of environments, he recognised the distinct phases they go through, and suggested they need to experience all four stages before they achieve maximum effectiveness. He refined and developed the model in 1977 (in conjunction with Mary Ann Jensen) with the addition of a fifth stage. Since then, others have attempted to adapt and extend the model - although sometimes with more of an eye on rhyme than reason. The phases are not to be perceived as sequential, because groups are messy, and cycle through the phases throughout their process.

Stage 1: Forming

Orientation (Forming) : This is simply the bringing together of a group of individuals. At this stage, members are: moderately eager, have generally positive expectations, have some anxiety about why they are there and what it all means and last but not the least have some anxiety about other members such as who they are and what they are like.

During orientation, the work output is generally low as members are focused on defining the goals and task, how to approach it, and what skills are needed. The length of this stage will depend on how clearly the task is defined. Groups with simple tasks will move through orientation quickly, but groups with complex goals and tasks may spend much longer in this stage.

This is an important stage because it serves to clarify the team's mission and bond team members. Teams that pay attention to building the relationships as well as focusing on the task tend to do better than those that skip over relationship building. Teams, after all, are made up of people who must work cooperatively for a successful outcome.

In the *forming* stage, personal relations are characterised by dependence. Group members rely on safe, patterned behaviour and look to the group leader for guidance and direction. Group members have a desire for acceptance by the group and a need to know that the group is safe. They set about gathering impressions and data about the similarities and differences among them and forming preferences for future sub-grouping. Rules of behaviour seem to be to keep things simple and to avoid controversy. Serious topics and feelings are avoided. The major task functions also concern orientation. Members attempt to become oriented to the tasks as well as to one another. Discussion centers around defining the scope of the task, how to approach it, and other similar concerns.

Individual behaviour is driven by a desire to be accepted by others, and avoid controversy or conflict. Serious issues and feelings are avoided, and people focus on being busy with routines, such as team, organisation, who does what, when to meet, etc. But individuals are also gathering information and impressions - about each other, and about the scope of the task and how to approach it. This is a comfortable stage to be in, but the avoidance of conflict and threat means that not much work is done actually. To grow from this stage to the next, each member must relinquish the comfort of non-threatening topics and risk the possibility of conflict.

Sage 2: Storming

Dissatisfaction (Storming): The next stage, which Tuckman calls storming, is characterised by argument, conflict and a dip in morale. It results from differences between initial expectations and the reality of the situation as perceived by the members. Members may have varying opinions of what the group was to do and how to accomplish it. Members are also beginning to confront the differences in their personalities and values, a condition that is present anytime strangers meet. Members may feel anger or frustration with the task or with other members or may even resent the presence of formal leadership.

Generally, the dissatisfaction stage is relatively short. Some groups, however, may become stuck in this stage and continue to be both demoralised and relatively unproductive. In the worst cases, some groups never emerge from this stage and, if possible, disband in frustration.

Storming is characterised by competition and conflict in the personal-relations. Individuals in the group can only remain nice to each other for as long, as important issues are not addressed. Some people's patience will break early, and minor confrontations will arise that are quickly dealt with or glossed over. These may relate to the work of the group itself, or to roles and responsibilities within the group. Some will feel that it's good to be getting into the real issues, whilst others will wish to remain in the comfort and security of stage 1. Depending on the culture of the organisation and individuals, the conflict will be more or less suppressed, but it will be there, under the surface. To deal with the conflict, individuals may feel they are winning or losing battles, and will look for structural clarity and rules to prevent the conflict persisting.

As the group members attempt to organise for the task, conflict inevitably results in their personal relations. Individuals have to bend and mold their feelings, ideas, attitudes, and beliefs to suit the group organisation. Because of "fear of exposure" or "fear of failure," there will be an increased desire for structural clarification and commitment. Although conflicts may or may not surface as group issues, they do exist. Questions will arise about who is going to be responsible for what, what the rules are, what the reward system is, and what criteria for evaluation are. These reflect conflicts over leadership, structure, power, and authority.

There may be wide swings in members' behaviour based on emerging issues of competition and hostilities. Because of the discomfort generated during this stage, some members may remain completely silent while others attempt to dominate. In order to progress to the next stage, group members must move from a "testing and proving" mentality to a problem-solving mentality. The most important trait in helping groups to move on to the next stage seems to be the ability to listen.

Stage 3: Norming

Resolution (Norming): This stage in the group's development involves resolving of issues, setting up group processes, setting of group policies, procedures, and values and increasing production. Members resolve differences and clarify the mission and roles. Members are less dissatisfied as in the previous stage because they are now learning more about each other and how they will work together. They make progress toward their goals.

In Tuckman's norming stage, interpersonal relations are characterised by cohesion. As Stage 3 evolves, the "rules of engagement" for the group become established, and the scope of the group's tasks or responsibilities is clear and agreed. Having had their arguments, they now understand each other better, and can appreciate each other's skills and experience. Individuals listen to each other, appreciate and support each other, and are prepared to change pre-conceived views: they feel they are part of a cohesive, effective group. However, individuals have had to work hard to attain this stage, and may resist any pressure to change - especially from the outside - for fear that the group will break up, or revert to a storm.

Group members are engaged in active acknowledgment of all members' contributions, community building and maintenance, and solving of group issues. Members are willing to change their preconceived ideas or opinions on the basis of facts presented by other members, and they actively ask questions of one another. Leadership is shared, and cliques dissolve. When members begin to know-and identify with-one another, the level of trust in their personal relations contributes to the development of group cohesion. It is during this stage of development (assuming the group gets this far) that people begin to experience a sense of group belonging and a feeling of relief as a result of resolving interpersonal conflicts.

The major task function of stage three is the data flow between group members: They share feelings and ideas, solicit and give feedback to one another, and explore actions related to the task. Creativity is high. If this stage of data flow and cohesion is attained by the group members, their interactions are characterised by openness and sharing of information on both a personal and task level. They feel good about being part of an effective group. The major drawback of the norming stage is that members may begin to fear the inevitable future breakup of the group; they may resist change of any sort.

Many work groups live in the comfort of Norming, and are fearful of moving back into Storming, or forward into Performing. This will govern their behaviour towards each other, and especially their reaction to change.

Stage 4: Performing

The *performing* stage is not reached by all groups. If group members are able to evolve to stage four, their capacity, range, and depth of personal relations expand to true interdependence. In this stage, people can work independently, in subgroups, or as a total unit with equal facility. Their roles and authorities dynamically adjust to the changing needs of the group and individuals.

Stage four is marked by interdependence in personal relations and problem solving in the realm of task functions. By now, the group should be most productive. Individual members have become self-assuring, and the need for group approval is past. Members are both highly task oriented and highly people oriented. There is unity: group identity is complete, group morale is high, and group loyalty is intense.

The task function becomes genuine problem solving, leading toward optimal solutions and optimum group development. There is support for experimentation in solving problems and an emphasis on achievement. The overall goal is productivity through problem solving and work Group identity, loyalty and morale are all high, and everyone is equally task-orientated and people-orientated. This high degree of comfort means that all the energy of the group can be directed towards the task(s) in hand.

Tuckman's original work simply described the way he had observed groups evolve, whether they were conscious of it or not. But for us the real value is in recognising where a group is in the process, and helping it to move to the Perform stage. In the real world, groups are often forming and changing, and each time that happens, they can move to a different Tuckman Stage. A group might be happily Norming or Performing, but a new member might force them back into Storming. Seasoned leaders will be ready for this, and will help the group get back to Performing as quickly as possible.

Ten years after first describing the four stages, Bruce Tuckman revisited his original work and described another, final, stage:

Stage 5: Adjourning

Tuckman's final stage, ***adjourning***, involves the termination of task behaviours and disengagement from relationships. A planned conclusion usually includes recognition for participation and achievement and an opportunity for members to say personal goodbyes. Concluding a group can create some apprehension - in effect, a minor crisis. The termination of the group is a regressive movement from giving up control to giving up inclusion in the group. The most effective interventions in this stage are those that facilitate task termination and the disengagement process. This is about completion and disengagement, both from the tasks and the group members. Individuals will be proud of having achieved much and glad to have been part of such an enjoyable group. They need to recognise what they have done, and consciously move on. Some authors describe stage 5 as “Deforming and Mourning”, recognising the sense of loss felt by group members.

❒❒❒

Chapter 10

Giving and Receiving Feedback

> *"Feedback is the breakfast of champions."*
>
> **–Ken Blanchard**

What is the shortest word in the English language that contains the letters: abcdef? Answer is feedback. Feedback is one of the essential elements of good communication that we give or get. Sometimes, feedback is called "criticism," but this seriously limits its meaning. It is a way to let people know how effective they are in what they are trying to accomplish, or how they affect you. It provides a way for people to learn how they affect the world around them, and it helps us to become more effective. If we know how other people see us, we can overcome problems in how we communicate and interact with them.

The term "feedback" was borrowed from rocket engineering by Kurt Lewin, founder of laboratory education. A rocket sent into space contains a mechanism that sends signals back to Earth. On earth, a steering apparatus receives these signals, makes adjustments if the rocket is off target, and corrects its course. The group can be seen as such a steering mechanism, sending signals when group members are off target in terms of the goals they have set for themselves.

Feedback is a must for people who want to have honest relationships. A powerful and important means for communication, feedback connects us, and our behaviour, to the world around us. Of course, there are two sides to feedback: giving it, and receiving it. The process of giving and asking for feedback is probably the most important dimension of laboratory education. It is through feedback that we can learn to "see ourselves as others see us." This, of course, is not an easy task. Effectively giving and receiving feedback implies certain key ingredients; caring, trusting, acceptance, openness, and a concern for the needs of others. Thus, how evaluative, judgmental, or helpful feedback is a skill that can be learnt and developed and for which certain useful guidelines exist.

Feedback is a reciprocal process; both senders and receivers can help each other in soliciting and in giving it. Sometimes it is also important to provide feedback on how a person is giving feedback. If a receiver is upset, hurt, or angry, other group members can say to the sender. "Look how you told him that; I would be angry, too" or "What other way could you have given him the same information without evaluating him or degrading him?" It is desirable to give feedback so that the receiver can preserve his self-esteem.

Receiving Feedback

Some people experience feedback as pure criticism and do not want to hear it. Others see it as spiritually crushing; a confirmation of their worthlessness. Still others only want to hear praise, but nothing that might suggest imperfection. That's not the case for everyone, of course. Some people are willing to accept feedback and seek it out, even if it is sometimes disturbing, because they believe they can grow from it.

It comes down to whether you believe feedback will harm you or benefit you. This is not to say that we should always have to accept feedback or the manner in which it is sometimes given. We all have the right to refuse feedback, and we can expect feedback to be given in a respectful and supportive manner.

Asking for feedback may indicate that the receiver is prepared to listen and wants to know how others perceive his behaviour. In asking for feedback, however, it is important to follow some of the same guidelines as for giving feedback. For example, a person should be specific about the subject on which he wants feedback. The individual who says to the group, I would like the group to tell me what they think about me" may receive

Exhibit 10.1 : Receiving Feedback

Negative/Closed Style	***Positive/Open Style***
Defensive: defends personal actions, frequently objects to feedback given.	***Open:*** listens without frequent interruption or objections.
Attacking: verbally attacks the feedback giver, and turns the table.	***Responsive:*** willing to hear what's being said without turning the table.
Denies: refutes the accuracy or fairness of the feedback.	***Accepting:*** accepts the feedback, without denial.
Disrespectful: devalues the speaker, what the speaker is saying, or the speaker's right to give feedback	***Respectful:*** recognises the value of what is being said and the speaker's right to say it.
Closed: ignores the feedback, listening blankly without interest.	***Engaged:*** interacts appropriately with the speaker, asks for clarification when needed.
Inactive listening: makes no attempt to "hear" or understand the meaning of the feedback.	***Active listening:*** listens carefully and tries to understand the meaning of the feedback.
Rationalising: finds explanations for the feedback that dissolves any personal responsibility.	***Thoughtful:*** tries to understand the personal behavior that has led to thefeedback.
Patronising: listens, but shows little interest.	***Interested:*** is genuinely interested in getting feedback.
Superficial: listens and agrees, but gives the impression that the feedback will have little actual effect.	*Sincere:* genuinely wants to make personal changes if appropriate

more feedback than he planned. In addition, the request is so general that the group members may be uncertain about where to begin or which behaviors are relevant to the request. In these cases, other group members can help the receiver by asking such questions as "Can you be more specific?"

Many people want to know how their behaviour is being perceived by other, but they fear the consequences of asking for such information. How easily a person will ask for feedback is related to the amount of the trust in the interpersonal relationship. However, people fear that the receiver will use their feedback (particularly negative feedback) to reinforce his feelings about himself. Again, it is sometimes difficult for a person to separate his behaviour from his feelings of self-worth.

There is a positive and open way of accepting feedback, but at the same time there is an opposite; a negative and closed manner which pushes feedback away and keeps it at bay.

Giving Feedback

The other end of feedback is giving it. Giving feedback effectively may depend on an individual's values and basic philosophy about himself, about his relationships with others, and about other people in general. Some people deliver feedback with relish; after all, it's easier to give advice than take it. Some use feedback as a weapon, or offer it as tit-for-tat. For others, feedback is a great way to be critical.

In most exchanges, feedback is usually imposed. People give feedback whether it is solicited or not and whether the person is prepared to receive it or not. In addition, the sender's need to give feedback may be much greater than the individual's need to receive it. This is particularly true when the sender is upset about something concerning the potential recipient. In many situations, it is legitimate to impose feedback, particularly when a norm exists for giving as well as for soliciting feedback, or in order to induce a norm of spontaneity. However, feedback is usually more helpful when the person solicits it.

Exhibit 10.2 : Giving Feedback

Negative feedback	***Positive feedback***
Imposed feedback	Solicited feedback
Feedback on Unmodifiable behaviour	Feedback on Modifiable behaviour
Feedback with Motivation to hurt	Feedback with Motivation to help
Feedback on Generalities	Feedback on specifics and data-based
Prescriptive Feedback	Suggestive Feedback
Evaluative Feedback	Non-Evaluative Feedback
Not immediate Feedback	Immediate Feedback

It is assumed that the primary motivation of membership in growth groups is to help one-self and others to grow. When an individual is angry, however, his motivation may be to hurt the other person. Frequently, the conflict turns into win-lose strategies in which the goals of the interaction are to degrade the other person. It is difficult when one is angry to consider that the needs of the other person are as important as his own. Angry feedback may be useless, even when the information is potentially helpful, because the receiver may need to reject the feedback in order to protect his integrity.

To be effective, feedback should be aimed at behaviour that is relatively easy to change. Many individuals' behaviours are habitual and could be described as a personal style developed through years of behaving and responding in certain ways. Feedback on this kind of behaviour often is frustrating because the behaviour can be very difficult to change.

Feedback on behaviours that are difficult to change may often make the person self-conscious and anxious about his behaviour. For example, if the wife of a chain smoker gives him feedback (using all of the appropriate guidelines) about his smoking, which is a behaviour determined by often-unknown causes. The individual may smoke to reduce his tension level; continuous feedback on his smoking behaviour may only increase his tension. Consequently, he smokes more to reduce that tension.

Occasionally, in giving feedback, one must determine whether the behaviour represents an individual's life style or results from some unknown personality factors. Sometimes it may be helpful first to ask the receiver whether he perceives his behaviour as modifiable. Many behaviours can be easily changed through feedback and the person's conscious desire to change his behaviour in order to produce more effective interpersonal style.

Avoid giving negative feedback in public. It is a good rule to criticise in private, praise in public **Focus on behaviour rather than attitude.** Avoid undue emotion– don't lose your cool or patience– over reacting will produce defensiveness. Talk when you are calm and objective.

General rules for giving feedback:

- Feedback should be non-threatening.
- Focus on the specific situation here and now, don't make broad generalisations or focus on the past.
- Do not give feedback if it is not requested, usable, and if it is not likely to result in the person feeling better about him/her and about you.
- Good feedback to another person focuses on his/her strengths, not faults.
- Provide specifics, not generalities.
- Provide feedback as soon as possible after the observed behaviour.
- Check for understanding an agreement with the recipient.
- Focus on observed behaviours not personality.
- Provide examples of the observed behaviour
- Provide suggestions, support and resources for improvement and change.
- Provide follow-up feedback to reinforce changes and to discuss changes that have *not* occurred.

Conclusion

The process of giving and receiving feedback obviously would be hampered if one attempted to consider all of the above guidelines. Some are needed more frequently than others: *i.e.,* feedback should be descriptive, non-evaluative, specific and should embody freedom of choice. These guidelines can also be used diagnostically. For example, when the person receiving feedback reacts defensively, some of the guidelines have probably been violated. Group members can ask the receiver how he heard the feedback and help the giver assess how he gave it.

Certain guidelines, however, can be learned and are valuable in helping people give and receive effective and useful feedback. To conclude *Effective Feedback* is:

1. **Supportive:** delivered in a non-threatening and encouraging manner.
2. **Direct:** the focus of the feedback is clearly stated.
3. **Sensitive:** delivered with sensitivity to the needs of the other person.
4. **Considerate:** feedback is intended to not insult or demean.
5. **Descriptive:** focuses on behaviour that can be changed, rather than personality.
6. **Specific:** feedback is focused on specific behaviours or events.
7. **Healthy timing:** given as close to the prompting event as possible and at an opportune time.
8. **Thoughtful:** well considered rather than impulsive.
9. **Helpful:** feedback is intended to be of value to the other person.

Avoid historical references. Present information on "here and now" as opposed to "there and then"

❑❑❑

Chapter 11

Sympathy versus Empathy

> *"The great gift of human beings is that we have the power of empathy."*
>
> **–Meryl Streep**
> **American Film Actress, 1949**

Empathy is the ability to not only detect what others feel; but also to experience that emotion yourself. This can be both a bane and a boon. If you can read another person's emotions then you can both avoid making a faux pas and also utilise their state to move them in another direction. When people are in emotional states their ability to decide is often significantly impaired. Thus, you cannot expect aroused people to make rational choices at this time. Empathy is a bane if you end up experiencing all the bad feelings of everyone around you. This is one of the problems that therapists and other counsellors have to handle.

Empathy is different from sympathy. Empathy *involves listening*; sympathy *involves reacting.* When we empathise with others, *we understand their feelings without getting involved in them.* When we sympathise with others, however, we *identify with their feelings to the point where we take on their pain.* The empathetic person asks questions; the sympathetic person may be moved to offer advice and solutions rather than allowing others to come to their own realisations. We are not meant to suffer when other do; their suffering can aid their growth. But we are meant to be there for others with a loving and supportive heart. The highest gift we can give others in a chance to express themselves at and to reach their own-not our-conclusion.

Empathy and sympathy are very close and are sometimes used as synonyms. The easiest way to separate them is to remember that empathy is about *feelings* whilst sympathy is about *actions*. Thus, you may empathise with another person and then act on this by telling them how sorry or happy you feel for them. Empathetic people are often very sympathetic - they can hardly stop themselves as they really do feel for the other person. A person who is sympathetic but not empathetic may appear a little shallow, as they are less likely to show an emotional connection. 'Terribly sorry and all that, old chap' they might say, in a friendly but relatively cold voice.

The value of empathy comes not from understanding the other person's feelings, but what you do as a result of this. Empathy connects people together. When you empathise with me, my sense of identity is connected to yours. As a result, I feel greater in some way and less alone. I may well, as a result, also start to empathise more with you. In any situation, having someone else really understand how you feel can be a blessed relief, as people with emotional problems often feel very much alone in their differentness from other people. The non-judgmental quality can also be very welcome.

Empathy displayed can be surprising and confusing. When not expected, it can initially cause suspicion, but when sustained it is difficult not to appreciate the concern. Empathy thus quickly leads to trust.

Empathy closes the loop: Consider what would happen if you had no idea what the other person felt about your communications to them. You might say something, they hated it, and you continued as if they understood and agreed. Not much persuasion happening there! The more you can empathise, the more you can get immediate feedback on what they are experiencing of your communications with them. And as a consequence, you can change what you are saying and doing to get them to feel what you want them to feel.

Distinction between empathy and sympathy is given in the following table:

Exhibit 11.1 : Sympathy versus Empathy

Sympathy = Enable	***Empathy = Empower***
When I am sympathetic:	**When I am empathetic:**
I feel responsible for others.	I feel responsible to others.
I fix.	I show empathy.
I protect.	I respect.
I rescue.	I listen.
I control.	I encourage.
I carry their feelings.	I share.
I don't listen.	I confront.
I feel tired.	I am at their level.
I feel anxious.	I am sensitive.
I feel fearful.	I feel relaxed.
I feel liable.	I feel free.
I am a manipulator.	I am a helper-guide.
I am concerned with the solution.	I am concerned with the person.
I am concerned with the answers.	I am concerned with the feelings.
I am concerned with the details.	I am concerned with relating person to person.
I am concerned with being right.	I believe if.
I am concerned with the performance.	I just share myself, the other person has
I am concerned with the circumstances	enough to make it.
I expect the person to live up to my expectations.	I expect the person to be responsible for himself and his own actions.
I can't let go.	I can trust and let go.

So how do you find out what other people are feeling? All you have to do is observe 'what they say, how they say it and what they do', which can also be described as 'words, music and dance'. If you want to move someone, detecting their emotional state is the first step. If you can feel that state then that detection is even more accurate. When you can sense their emotion, you can then use this to move them in the direction you want them to take.

The trick in spotting feelings is to pay close attention to changes in the other person in response to external events. If you say 'How are you?' and the corners of their mouth turn down and their voice tone goes flat, then you might detect that all is not well. The better you are at spotting small changes, the greater your potential ability at empathising. Watch for small changes on the face. Watch for lower-body movements when the upper-body is under conscious control. Listen for tension in the voice and emphasis on specific words. Listen for emotional words.

To avoid getting swamped by their emotions learn to dip in and out of the association that makes you feel what they do. Go in, test the temperature and then get out to a place where you can think more rationally. Unless you are really sure, it can be a good idea to reflect back to the other person what you are sensing of their feelings, to check that you have got it right. After all, the only person who can confirm empathy is the person whose emotions are being sensed.

Reflecting back itself has an effect, typically leading the other person to appreciate that you really care about them and hence increasing their trust in you. Empathy is far more effective when it is offered, as opposed to when people ask for empathy (in which case a negotiation exchange dynamic is set up).

Chapter 12

Thinking versus Feeling

> *"Every portrait that is painted with feeling is a portrait of the artist, not of the sitter."*
>
> **–Oscar Wilde**
> **(Irish Poet, Novelist, Dramatist and Critic, 1854-1900)**

Thinking and Feeling are one of the preferences used in the *Jungian Type Inventory* and two major ways to which we interact with our interpersonal environment. Both are essential to constructive communication. The naming is unfortunately a bit archaic as thinking is more than thought, and feeling is not about being over-emotional or fluffy. They are about how we decide: through logic or through considering people. In general, thinking ("head talk") leads to an explanation of the interactive situation, while feeling ("gut talk") leads to an understanding of it. As someone has said, "Head talk is the prose of communication while gut talk is the poetry of communication."

Thinking

Thinkers decide based primarily on logic, and when they do so, they consider a decision to be made. They tend to see the world in black and white and dislike fuzziness. Perhaps because people are so variable, they focus on tangible things, seeking truth and use of clear rules. At work, they are task-oriented, seek to create clear value. Interacting with them tends to be brief and business-like. They may be seen as cold and heartless by feelers.

"Think statements refer to the denotative aspects of the environment. They attempt to define, assert, opine, rationalise, or make casual connections between environment events. Thinking statements are bound by the logic and scientific enquiry; they may be true or untrue. We are constantly engaged in cognitive work: observing, inferring, categorising, generalising, and summarising: occasionally we report to others what goes on in our head. Frequently, we are asked for facts, speculation or, sometimes, just a "what are you thinking about?"

Feeling

Feelers decide based primarily through social considerations, listening to their heart and considering the feelings of others. They see life as a human existence and material things as being subservient to this. They value harmony and use tact in their interactions with others. At work, they are sociable and people-oriented and make many decisions based on values (more than value). They may be seen as unreliable and emotional by Thinkers.

"Feel statements refer to the connotative aspects of the environment. They attempt to report our internal affective, immediate, not rational, emotional, "gut" response to environmental events. Usually, feel statements are personal as they refer to inner states of human beings, what's happening inside of us. Feel statements, like dreams, cannot be true or false, good or bad, but only honestly or dishonestly communicated. Feel statements may not require words at all.

Laboratory training to differentiate between Thinking and Feeling

Laboratory learning places great emphasis on feelings. Many participants in groups learn quickly that beginning sentences with "I think" is bad form, so they preface their remarks with "I feel" and go on to report thoughts. This bogus use of "I feel" often muddles communication.

1. "I feel like having a drink" is no expression of feeling but merely a shorthand way of saying. "I'm thinking about having a drink, but I'm still undecided. "Here, "feel" is used to express an indefinite thought.

2. "I feel that Roger's brashness is a cover for his insecurity" is not an expression of feeling but a statement of opinion, an offering of an hypothesis.

3. "I feel that all men are created equal". An abstract principle can's really be felt: this is a statement of belief that all men are created equal".

4. Watch yourself when you say "I feel that..." It's a tip-off that you are making a think statement with a feel prefix.

Many of us have conditioned ourselves to screen out awareness of internal reactions. We may allow ourselves to report feeling "interested" or "uncomfortable" but deny ourselves more intense or varied reactions. Laboratory learning emphasises feeling states precisely because of this conditioning and denial. By getting in touch with our inner events, we enrich our experiences with the reality surrounding us.

Taking Responsibility for Your Thoughts and Feelings

Effective communication occurs when the communicators take responsibility for their thoughts, feelings and overt behaviour. Blaming, imputing motives are sneaky, dishonest attempts to be irresponsible. When you own your thoughts and feelings, the other person knows where you are and can respond more authentically to you. You are entitled to have thoughts and feelings in your interpersonal environment. Being aware of them and the differences between them can improve your communications.

Changes inside us provide direct cues to the feelings we are experiencing. A change in bodily functioning – muscle tighten, restlessness, frowning, smiling, inability to stay with conversation – tells us how we are reacting to what is happening. Sometimes we can also become aware of what is blocking our awareness of what we are experiencing. Shame is one kind of block, especially when the impulse sounds childish or regressive. In a well- functioning group, these blocks do not correspond to reality. It can be truly liberating to express your feeling without shame, fear, or judgment.

Feelers or Thinkers

Taking into consideration the difference between feelers and thinkers, both need to be dealt differently. So while dealing with feelers and thinkers, following points need to be considered :

Exhibit 12.1 : Feelers or Thinkers

With thinkers	*With feelers*
Be brief and concise.	Introduce yourself and get to know the person; full acceptance may take considerable amount of time.
Be logical; don't ramble without any apparent purpose.	Be personable and friendly.
Be intellectually critical and objective.	Demonstrate empathy by showing areas of agreement first.
Be calm and reasonable.	Show how the idea will affect people and what people's reaction would be.
Don't assume that feelings are unimportant; they may have a different value.	Be aware that how you communicate is as important as what you're communicating.
Present feelings and emotions as additional facts to be weighed in a decision.	Let them talk about personal impact; accept decisions that may not be based on facts.

Example:

Ram and Shyam both work in the same company. Ram stops and talks to everyone. People find him friendly, willing to listen to their troubles and encouraging. Shyam is quite different. He stays focused on his work, tends not to get involved in people's troubles, but tends to have a cleared desk by the end of the day. Shyam thinks that a lot of Ram's socialising is a waste of time, but he is sometimes envious that Ram knows and is liked by everyone. Ram thinks that Shyam is too serious, but secretly is envious of his effectiveness and clear thinking. Each one thinks that he brings a lot of gifts to the company and has great hopes of great personal success.

However, who will be most effective in their job largely depends not so much on their own personality type, but on the personality type of the company. Is the company more *thinking* (logical) or *feeling* (values) oriented? This is a common problem for many people. What kind of workplace are you in and how well do you fit there? Finding a comfortable fit between our personality and our workplace often takes us years to achieve. Many people just give up and struggle to survive.

Exhibit 12.2 : Thinking and Feeling Companies

Thinking (head) companies tend to	*Feeling or heart companies tend to*
Function in terms of rules and regulations.	Make their decisions based on company values.
Believe that criticism tends to lead to efficiency.	Think and function in terms of specific human situations.
Emphasise an objective approach to things.	Believe that support leads to employees being more effective.
Decide on the basis of principles.	Emphasise the importance of people and their concerns.

The problem is that like head or heart people, head or heart companies tend to distrust the other side. So *thinking* companies like business, manufacturing, the police or military tend to distrust their own *feeling*, value oriented side, so they tend to distrust the *feeling* people in the company. Heart people tend to feel marginalised, discounted, and pushed out of the corridors of power. Also, when *feeling* types have to deal with the powers that be, they may find them hard, unfeeling, and rule oriented. The example that comes to my mind is the way police departments traditionally dealt with people who were sexually assaulted. Here you tend to have one mostly thinking organisation (the police) reinforced by another predominantly thinking organisation (the law), trying to deal with very emotional, fragile people and perhaps not doing the best job of it. Many people have said it would have made more sense not to complain, because they just felt assaulted again.

On top of that, heart people tend to find it very hard to articulate an argument that will persuade the thinking departmental managers to attend to values. Head companies tend to continue as head companies. For example, how many heart people have you heard about who have been broken by the military because they were not tough enough and able to take criticism? Taking criticism tends to be one of the enduring ideals of thinking companies. *Suck it up, Deal with it, Tough it out,* are *thinking* kinds of criticism.

Business is predominantly a *thinking* (head) activity, though there are some *feeling* (head) companies. A more *feeling* company would be something like a community centre. There has been a great deal of criticism lately about the predominantly *thinking*, traditionally male, approach to business, claiming that it is responsible for an environmentally insensitive, money first/people last business approach. I find the most successful and balanced businesses tend to be the ones where the company has developed both sides of itself, head and heart, just as many of the happiest, most successful people have developed both of those sides in themselves.

The conflict between feeling and thinking are a good illustration of the problem of decision-making. Both viewpoints have validity. Jung said that wisdom was the integration of thinking and feeling. By this he did not mean that the conflict between them could be resolved. He only meant that a wise individual is able to use either function as the situation demanded. It's not a matter of being aware of subjective and objective issues. That is all thinking. It is a matter of shifting functions and standpoints.

❑❑❑

Part Three

Theories and Models of Human Processes

Chapter 13

Kolb's Learning Cycle

> *"Nothing ever becomes real till it is experienced".*
>
> **— John Keats**

This oft-repeated quote of Confucius is perhaps the best analogy of experiential learning. We take in information through our senses, yet we ultimately learn by doing. First, we watch and listen to others. Then we try doing things on our own. This sparks our interest and generates our motivation to self-discover.

Think back on learning to ride a bicycle, use a computer, dance, or sing. We took an action, saw the consequences of that action, and chose either to continue, or to take a new and different action. What allowed us to master the new skill was our active participation in the event and our reflection on what we attained. Experience and reflection taught more than any book or lecture ever could.

In the book *Experiential Learning,* David Kolb describes learning as a four-step process. He identifies the steps as (1) watching and (2) thinking (mind), (3) feeling (emotion), and (4) doing (muscle). Kolb wrote that learners have immediate concrete experiences that allow us to reflect on new experience from different perspectives. From these reflective observations, we engage in abstract conceptualisation, creating generalisations or principles that integrate our observations into sound theories. Finally, we use these generalisations or theories as guides to further action. Active experimentation allows us to test what we learn in new and more complex situations. The result is another concrete experience, but this time at a more complex level.

To be effective learners we must *(1) receive information, (2) reflect on how it will impact some aspect of our life, (3) compare how it fits into our own experiences, and (4) think about how this information offers new ways for us to act.* Learning requires more than seeing, hearing, moving, or touching to learn. We integrate what we sense and think with what we feel and how we behave. Without that integration, we're just passive participants and passive learning alone doesn't engage our higher brain functions or stimulate our senses to the point where we integrate our lessons into our existing schemes. We must do something with our knowledge.

'Teaching by pouring in' refers to a medieval belief that we could teach people by drilling holes in the human head and, with a funnel, pour information into the brain. Though we now snicker at that model, we use equally absurd methods today. As long as professors model passive learning to future teachers/trainers as acceptable and useful, instructors will be unprepared and unwilling to use other techniques such as experiential learning.

Likewise, because many of us have not seen other techniques, we do not know what we are missing. Active learning results in longer-term recall, synthesis, and problem-solving skills than learning by hearing, reading, or watching. Indian education needs to move from a learning-by-telling model and even learning-by-observing (as in the case-method) to a learning-by-doing model. We must move from passivity to activity. We must learn to extrapolate from our experiences and see how to apply what we have done to new instances.

The main reason educational or training institutes have not integrated experiential-focused theories into all instruction remains a lack of understanding why and how learning-by-doing works. Educators may recognise that experience teaches real-life skills, but they do not see the connection to learning facts. Most teachers/trainers still follow the drill-them-and-test-them school of educational thought.

The problem with experiential learning is that in organisations we may not get to see the outcomes of our actions and, thus, cannot reflect on them to learn. The consequences of our actions may be in the too distant future or affect a part of the organisation far removed from ours. As Peter Senge said "We each have a learning horizon, a breadth of vision in time and space within which we assess our effectiveness". When our actions have consequences beyond our learning horizon, it becomes impossible to learn from direct experience. Herein lies the core learning dilemma that confronts organisations [and thus individuals]. We learn best from experience, but we never directly experience the consequences of many of our most important decisions.

The Theory of Experiential Learning

David A. Kolb developed a theory of experiential learning called The Kolb Cycle, The Learning Cycle or The Experiential Learning Cycle. The cycle comprises four different stages of learning from experience to action and can be entered at any point but all stages must be followed in sequence for successful learning to take place. The Learning Cycle suggests that it is not sufficient to have an experience in order to learn. It is necessary to reflect on the experience to make generalisations and formulate concepts which can then be applied to new situations. This learning must then be tested out in new situations. The learner must make the link between the theory and action by planning, acting out, reflecting and relating it back to the theory.

Kolb, in his book *"Experiential Learning"* (1984) proposed a Theory of Experiential Learning in which he identifies four principal stages: Concrete Experiences (CE), Reflective Observation (RO), Abstract Conceptualisation (AC), and Active Experimentation (AE). The CE/AC and AE/RO dimensions are polar opposites in terms of learning styles, and

Kolb suggests four types of learners: Divergers, Assimilators, Convergers, and Accommodators, depending upon their position on these two dimensions.

Experiential learning occurs as a direct result of the learner's participation in events, it utilises the participants' own experience and their own reflection about that experience. It is a learner centered approach which starts with the promise that people learn best from experience (learning-by-doing). It is particularly effective due to its holistic approach of addressing cognitive, emotional and the physical aspect of the learner.

Experiential learning is characterised by the following:

- Recognises that people learn best from their own experiences and their own reviews.
- Subscribes to the notion that what people do is more important than what they know.
- Moves beyond knowledge and into skill by generating a learning experience.
- Understands that to be remembered over a long period of time the learning process should be enjoyable, motivating and rewarding.
- Respects the individual's ideas and choices.
- Provides opportunity to take on challenge in an atmosphere of support.
- Generates space and time to stand back and reflect when pressures or doubts become too strong.
- Cultivates a realisation that the attempt at doing something new or different is more significant than the result.
- Produces awareness that effective learning requires small controlled steps outside comfort zones.

Kolb's model therefore works on two levels - *a four-stage cycle and four-types of learning styles.*

Exhibit 13.1 : Learning Cycle

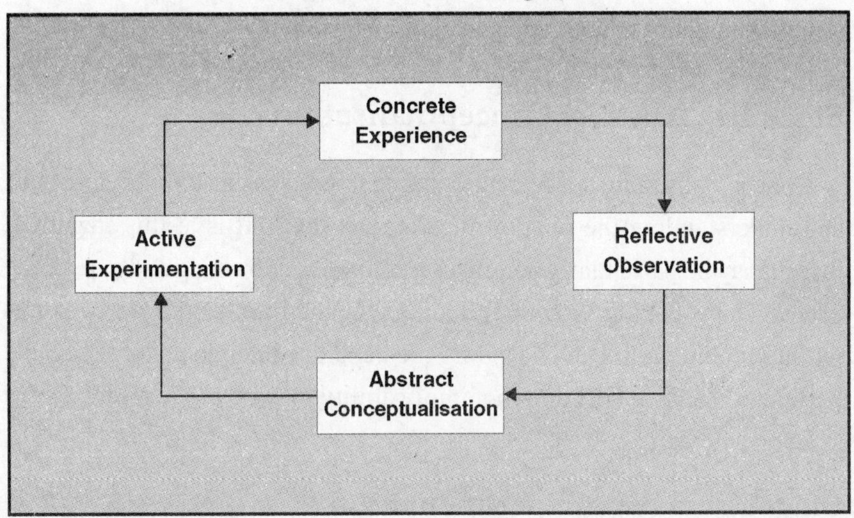

Learning Cycle

The learning cycle has been determined by observing that learning invariably follows a pattern that can be divided into four stages. Kolb argues that the learning cycle can begin at any one of the four points however, the following is the most often suggested pattern for the learning process:

Stage I: Concrete Experience

An individual carries out a particular action and then observes the effect of the action in this situation. Experiencing or immersing oneself in the "doing" of a task is the stage in which the learner simply carries out the task assigned. The engaged person is usually not reflecting on the task at this time but rather just carrying it out with intention.

Stage II : Reflective Observation

Reflection involves stepping back from task involvement and reviewing what has been done and experienced. The skills of attending, noticing differences, and applying terms helps identify subtle events. One's paradigm (values, attitudes, beliefs) influences whether one can differentiate certain events. Understanding of the effects of an action in the particular instance is required in order to anticipate what would follow from the action if it was to be taken again under the same circumstances.

Stage III : Abstract Conceptualisation

Conceptualisation involves interpreting the events that have been noticed and understanding the relationships among them. It is at this stage that theory may be particularly helpful as a template for framing and explaining events. One's paradigm again influences the interpretive range a person is willing to entertain. Understanding the general principle under which the particular instance falls does not imply ability to express the principle in a symbolic medium.

Stage IV : Active Experimentation

Active Experimentation is application through action in a new circumstance within the range of generalisation. Within this context planning enables taking the new understanding and translates it into predictions about what is likely to happen next or what actions should be taken to refine the way the task is handled.

The timing of the Learning cycle is considered to be particularly important. On the one hand, if one waits until after a task is completed there is no opportunity to refine it until a similar task arises; on the other hand, continual reflection leaves the person spending more time on thinking than getting the task done. The logic of the learning cycle is to make many small and incremental improvements.

Two aspects of the Learning Cycle can be seen as especially noteworthy: the use of concrete, *'here-and-now' experience* to test ideas; and *use of feedback* to change practices and theories.

Learning Styles

Cognitive styles or Learning styles could be defined as an individual's orientation for approaching learning tasks, or preferred way in which a learner processes information. Learning styles characterise a person's typical manner of thinking, remembering or problem solving, they simply denote a tendency to behave in a certain manner, and they are considered to be bipolar dimensions. Learning styles are based on two dimensions : Preference dimension and Perception dimension.

Preference dimension: In the vertical preference, dimension, people will have a preference along the continuum between:

- *Concrete experience*: Looking at things as they are, without any change, in raw detail, and
- *Abstract conceptualisation*: Looking at things as concepts and ideas, after a degree of processing that turns the raw detail into an internal model.

People who prefer concrete experience will argue that thinking about something changes it, and that direct empirical data is essential. Those who prefer abstraction will argue that meaning is created only after internal processing and that idealism is a more real approach. This spectrum is very similar to the Jungian scale of *Sensing* vs. *Intuiting*.

Exhibit 13.2: Preference and Processing Dimensions of Learning Styles

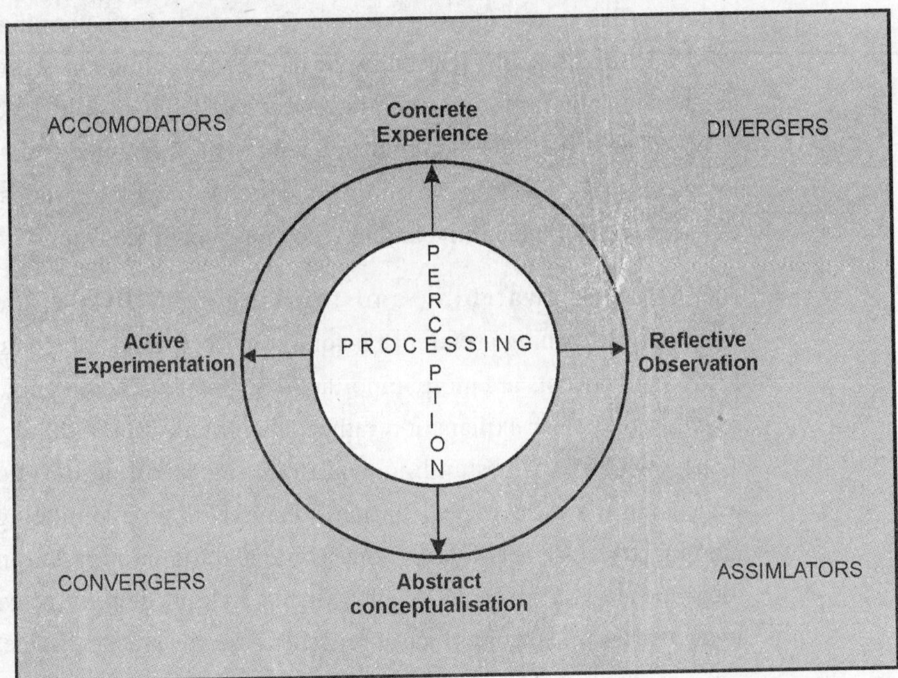

Processing dimension: In the horizontal processing dimension, people will take the results of their perception and process it in preferred ways along the continuum between:

- *Active experimentation*: Taking what they have concluded and trying it out to prove that it works.
- *Reflective observation*: Taking what they have concluded and watching to see if it works.

Descriptions of Four Kolb Learning Styles

Below is given brief descriptions of the four Kolb learning styles:

- **Diverging (feeling and watching - CE/RO) :** These people are able to look at things from different perspectives. They are sensitive. They prefer to watch rather than do, tending to gather information and use imagination to solve problems. They are best at viewing concrete situations several different viewpoints. Kolb called this style 'diverging' because these people perform better in situations that require ideas-generation, for example, brainstorming. People with a diverging learning style have broad cultural interests and like to gather information. They are interested in people, tend to be imaginative and emotional, and tend to be strong in the arts. People with the diverging learning style prefer to work in groups, to listen with an open mind and to receive personal feedback.
- **Assimilating (watching and thinking - AC/RO) :** The assimilating learning preference is for a concise, logical approach. Ideas and concepts are more important than people. These people require good clear explanation rather than practical opportunity. They excel at understanding wide-ranging information and organising it a clear logical format. People with an assimilating learning style are less focused on people and more interested in ideas and abstract concepts. People with this style are more attracted to logically sound theories than approaches based on practical value.

These learning style people are important for effectiveness in information and science careers. In formal learning situations, people with this style prefer readings, lectures, exploring analytical models, and having time to think things through.

- **Converging (doing and thinking - AC/AE) :** People with a converging learning style can solve problems and will use their learning to find solutions to practical issues. They prefer technical tasks, and are less concerned with people and interpersonal aspects. People with a converging learning style are best at finding practical uses for ideas and theories. They can solve problems and make decisions by finding solutions to questions and problems. People with a converging learning style are more attracted to technical tasks and problems than social or interpersonal issues. A converging learning style enables specialist and technology abilities. People with a converging style like to experiment with new ideas, to simulate, and to work with practical applications.
- **Accommodating (doing and feeling - CE/AE) :** The accommodating learning style is 'hands-on', and relies on intuition rather than logic. These people use other people's analysis, and prefer to take a practical, experiential approach. They are attracted to new challenges and experiences, and to carrying out plans. They commonly act on 'gut' instinct rather than logical analysis. People with an accommodating learning style will tend to rely on others for information than carry out their own analysis. This learning style is prevalent and useful in roles requiring action and initiative. People with an accommodating learning style prefer to work in teams to complete tasks. They set targets and actively work in the field trying different ways to achieve an objective.

As with any behavioural model, this is a guide not a strict set of rules. Nevertheless most people clearly exhibit clear strong preferences for a given learning style. The ability to use or 'switch between' different styles is not one that we should assume comes easily or naturally to many people. Simply, people who have a clear learning style preference, for whatever

Exhibit 13.3 : Learning Styles

	Doing (Active Experimentation – AE)	*Watching (Reflective Observation –RO)*
Feeling (Concrete Experience - CE)	**Accommodating (CE/AE)**	**Diverging (CE/RO)**
Thinking (Abstract Conceptualisation – AC)	**Converging (AC/AE)**	**Assimilating (AC/RO)**

reason, will tend to learn more effectively if learning is orientated according to their preference. For instance, people who prefer the 'assimilating' learning style will not be comfortable being thrown in at the deep end without notes and instructions. or people who like prefer to use an 'accommodating' learning style are likely to become frustrated if they are forced to read lots of instructions and rules, and are unable to get hands on experience as soon as possible.

❑❑❑

Chapter 14

Johari Window: A Model of Self-Awareness

> *"The final mystery is oneself."*
> **–Oscar Wilde**

Johari Window model is a simple and useful tool for illustrating and improving self-awareness, and mutual understanding between individuals within a group. The Johari Window tool can also be used to assess and improve a group's relationship with other groups. The Johari Window model was developed by American psychologists Joseph Luft and Harry Ingham in the 1950's, while researching group dynamics. Today the Johari Window model is especially relevant due to modern emphasis on, and influence of, 'soft' skills, behaviour, empathy, cooperation, inter-group development and interpersonal development.

Interestingly, Joe Luft and Harry Ingham called their Johari Window model 'Johari' after combining their first names, Joe and Harry. In early publications the word actually appears as 'JoHari'. The Johari Window soon became a widely used model for understanding and training self-awareness, personal development, improving communications, interpersonal relationships, group dynamics, team development and inter-group relationships.

The Johari Window model is also referred to as a 'disclosure/feedback model of self-awareness, and by some people an 'information processing tool'. The Johari Window actually represents information - feelings, experience, views, attitudes, skills, intentions, motivation, etc - within or about a person - in relation to their group, from four perspectives. The Johari Window model can also be used to represent the same information for a group in relation to other groups. Johari Window terminology refers to 'self' and 'others': 'self' means oneself, *i.e.,* the person subject to the Johari Window analysis and 'others' means other people in the person's group or team.

When the Johari Window model is used to assess and develop groups in relation to other groups, the 'self' would be the group, and 'others' would be other groups. However, for ease of explanation and understanding of the Johari Window and examples in this article, think of the model applying to an individual within a group, rather than a group relating to other groups.

The four Johari Window perspectives are called 'regions' or 'areas' or 'quadrants'. Each of these regions contains and represents the information - feelings, motivation, etc - known about the person, in terms of whether the information is known or unknown by the person, and whether the information is known or unknown by others in the group.

Like some other behavioural models *eg.,* Tuckman, Hersey/Blanchard), the Johari Window is based on a four-square grid - the Johari Window is like a window with four 'panes'. Here's how the Johari Window is normally shown, with its four regions, as shown in Exhibit 14.1.

Exhibit 14.1: Johari Window's Four Regions

	Known to Self	***Not Known to Self***
Known to Others	Arena/open area	Blind area
Not Known to Others	Closed area	Dark area

Quadrant 1 : 'Open Self/Area' or 'Free Area' or 'Public Area', or 'Arena'

Johari region 1 is also known as the 'area of free activity'. This is the information about the person - behaviour, attitude, feelings, emotion, knowledge, experience, skills, views, etc - *known by the person* ('the self') and *known by the group* ('others').

The aim in any group should always be to develop the 'open area' for every person, because when we work in this area with others we are at our most effective and productive and the group is at its most productive too. The open free area, or 'the arena', can be seen as the space where good communications and cooperation occur, free from distractions, mistrust, confusion, conflict and misunderstanding.

Established team members logically tend to have larger open areas than new team members. New team members start with relatively small open areas because relatively little knowledge about the new team member is shared. *The size of the open area can be expanded horizontally into the blind space, by seeking and actively listening to feedback from other group members. This process is known as 'feedback solicitation'.* Also, other group members can help a team member expand their open area by offering feedback, sensitively of course. *The size of the open area can also be expanded vertically downwards into the hidden or avoided space by the person's disclosure of information, feelings, etc about him/herself to the group and group members.* Also, group members can help a person expand their open area into the hidden area by asking the person about him/herself.

Managers and team leaders can play an important role in facilitating feedback and disclosure among group members, and in directly giving feedback to individuals about their own blind areas. Leaders also have a big responsibility to promote a culture and expectation for open, honest, positive, helpful, constructive, sensitive communications, and the sharing of knowledge throughout their organisation. Top performing groups, departments, companies and organisations always tend to have a culture of open positive communication, so encouraging the positive development of the 'open area' or 'open self' for everyone is a simple yet fundamental aspect of effective leadership.

Quadrant 2 : 'Blind Self' or 'Blind Area' or 'Blind Spot'

Johari region 2 is what is *known* about a person by others in the group, but is *unknown* by the person him/hcrsclf. The aim should be to reduce this area and thereby to increase the open area (*i.e.,* to increase self-awareness), by seeking or soliciting feedback from others. This blind area is not an effective or productive space for individuals or groups. This blind area could also be referred to as ignorance about oneself, or issues in which one is deluded. A blind area could also include issues that others are deliberately withholding from a person. We all know how difficult it is to work well when kept in the dark. People who are 'thick-skinned' tend to have a large 'blind area'.

Group members and managers can take some responsibility for helping an individual to reduce their blind area - in turn increasing the open area - *by giving sensitive feedback and encouraging disclosure.* Managers should promote a climate of non-judgmental feedback, and group response to individual disclosure, which reduces fear and therefore encourages both processes to happen. The extent to which an individual seeks feedback, and the issues on which feedback is sought, must always be at the individual's own discretion. Some people are more resilient than others - care needs to be taken to avoid causing emotional upset.

Quadrant 3 : 'Hidden Self' or 'Hidden Area' or 'Avoided Self/Area' or 'Facade'

Johari region 3 is what is *known to ourselves* but kept hidden from, and therefore *unknown, to others.* This hidden or avoided self represents information, feelings, etc, anything that a person knows about him/self, but which is not revealed or is kept hidden from others. The hidden area could also include sensitivities, fears, hidden agendas, manipulative intentions and secrets - anything that a person knows but does not reveal, for whatever reason. It's natural for very personal and private information and feelings to remain hidden.

Relevant hidden information and feelings, etc, should be moved into the open area through the *process of 'disclosure'*. The aim should be to disclose and expose relevant information and feelings, thereby increasing the open area. By telling others how we feel and other information about ourselves we reduce the hidden area, and increase the open area, which enables better understanding, cooperation, trust, team-working effectiveness and productivity. Reducing hidden areas also reduces the potential for confusion, misunderstanding, poor communication, etc, which all distract from and undermine team effectiveness.

Organisational culture and working atmosphere have a major influence on group members' preparedness to disclose their hidden selves. Most people fear judgment or vulnerability and therefore hold back hidden information and feelings. The extent to which an individual discloses personal feelings and information, and the issues which are disclosed, and to whom, must always be at the individual's own discretion. Some people are more keen and able than others to disclose. People should disclose at a pace and depth that they find personally comfortable. As with feedback, some people are more resilient than others - care needs to be taken to avoid causing emotional upset.

Quadrant 4 : 'Unknown Self' or 'Unknown Area'

Johari region 4 contains information, feelings, latent abilities, aptitudes, experiences etc, that are *unknown to the person* him/herself and *unknown to others in the group.* These unknown issues take a variety of forms: they can be feelings, behaviours, attitudes, capabilities, aptitudes, which can be quite close to the surface, and which can be positive and useful, or they can be deeper aspects of a person's personality, influencing his/her behaviour to various degrees. Large unknown areas would typically be expected in younger people, and people who lack experience or self-belief.

Examples of unknown factors are as follows, and the first example is particularly relevant and common, especially in typical organisations and teams:

- An ability that is under-estimated or un-tried through lack of opportunity, encouragement, confidence or training.
- A natural ability or aptitude that a person does not realise they possess.
- A fear or aversion that a person does not know they have.
- An unknown illness.
- Repressed or subconscious feelings.
- Conditioned behaviour or attitudes from childhood.

The processes by which this information and knowledge can be uncovered are various, and can be prompted through self-discovery or observation by others, or in certain situations through collective or mutual discovery, of the sort of discovery experienced on outward bound courses or other deep or intensive group work. Counselling can also uncover unknown issues, but this would then be known to the person and by one other, rather than by a group.

Again as with disclosure and soliciting feedback, the process of self discovery is a sensitive one. The extent and depth to which an individual is able to seek out discover their unknown feelings must always be at the individual's own discretion. Some people are more keen and able than others to do this.

Managers and leaders can help by creating an environment that encourages self-discovery, and to promote the processes of self-discovery, constructive observation and feedback among team members. It is a widely accepted industrial fact that the majority of staff in any organisation are at any time working well within their potential. Creating a culture, climate and expectation for self-discovery helps people to fulfill more of their potential and thereby to achieve more, and to contribute more to organisational performance.

The unknown area could also include repressed or subconscious feelings rooted in formative events and traumatic past experiences, which can stay unknown for a lifetime. In a work or organisational context the Johari Window should not be used to address issues of a clinical nature.

❑❑❑

Chapter 15

Goleman's Theory of Emotional Intelligence

> *"Let's not forget that the little emotions are the great captains of our lives and we obey them without realising it".*
>
> **–Vincent Van Gogh, 1889**

Our perception of the relationship between thought and emotions turns out to be somewhat misguided. The majority of us subscribe to the idea that thought is most appropriate when not clouded by emotions. And, sure enough, strong emotions make it difficult to think straight. Rationalists have even made the elimination of emotion from thought their credo. Yet, clinical experiments show that thought devoid of emotions renders satisfactory decision-making impossible. The problem is not with emotions as such, but with the appropriateness of emotion and its expression. The task is not so much to suppress emotions, since every feeling has its value and significance, but to strike a balance between rational thoughts and emotions. One of the keys to sound decision-making is a greater awareness of our emotions and those of others. Emotions are not just present when we fly off the handle or jump for joy, but are omnipresent in the most subtle ways in all our acts. How often are we in the sway of our emotions without even realising it?

Emotional Intelligence

For many years, it was thought that a person's intelligence (IQ or intelligence quotient) determined how people succeeded in life. Schools used IQ tests to choose children for gifted programs and some companies even used IQ scores when hiring. In the last ten years, researchers have found that IQ is not the only predictor of a person's success. They are now looking at emotional intelligence (EQ) as another determinant of a person's success in life.

Emotional intelligence was popularised in 1995 when psychologist Daniel Goleman wrote his book, *Emotional Intelligence: Why It Can Matter More Than IQ*. Both types of intelligence are important but in different ways. The IQ contributes about 20% to the factors that determine life accomplishments. That leaves about 80% for everything else. Research has shown that emotional intelligence can make a difference in life's successes. For example, boys in the second grade who are impulsive and always getting into trouble are six to eight times more likely than other children to be violent in their teens and commit crimes. Sixth grade girls who confuse feelings of boredom and anger with hunger are the ones most likely to have eating disorders when they become teenagers. These children are unaware of how they are feeling and what it's called. So if a person does not have these skills, he or she can get into trouble, especially as a child transitions into adulthood.

Emotional, or social intelligence, involves at least five types of skills:

- **Self-awareness** is a person's ability to understand and be aware of their feelings and moods. Self-awareness helps a person keep an eye on their thoughts and emotions so they can better understand why they feel a particular way.
- **Managing emotions :** This skill helps people display their emotions in socially appropriate ways. It helps one control anger, sadness, and fear.
- **Motivation** helps a person use their emotions to reach their goals. It helps them hold back their impulses and delay gratification to reach these goals.

- **Empathy** is the ability to understand how a person feels. It is different from feeling sorry for someone. It is feeling like "walking in their shoes."
- **Social skills** are dealing with others in social situations. It is the ability to carry on a conversation and deal with other's emotions. It is being socially competent.

If a person does have these abilities or emotional intelligence, it will help him or her throughout life. These abilities affect everything from success in marriage to how well one does on the job. Emotional skills also help a person academically. Such skills as postponing gratification or enjoyment when searching for long-term goals are helpful to children academically. Children who can stick with tasks and finish homework or assignments do much better later in life than those children who are easily distracted and go off to do something else.

Many theorists criticise the way Goleman defines emotional intelligence. For them, emotional intelligence is the ability to understand how others' emotions work and to control one's own emotions. By comparison, Goleman defines emotional intelligence more broadly, also including such competencies as optimism, conscientiousness, motivation, empathy and social competence. These broader traits that Goleman relates to emotional intelligence are considered personality traits by other theorists.

Responding to such charges, Goleman says cognitive skill 'gets you in the door' of a company, but emotional skill helps you thrive once you are hired; for example, a Harvard business graduate received numerous job offers from companies clamoring to hire her. However, due to a lack of emotional intelligence, the woman continually sparred with her employers and could not keep any of the jobs.

Studies of close to 500 organisations worldwide, reviewed by Goleman in his book, indicate that people who score highest on EQ measures rise to the top of corporations. 'Star' employees possess more interpersonal skills and confidence, For example, than 'regular' employees who receive less glowing performance reviews. 'Emotional intelligence matters twice as much as technical and analytic skill combined for star performances,' he says. 'And the higher people move up in the company, the more crucial emotional intelligence becomes.'

EQ at Work

Expressing emotion is one of the trickiest workplace issues. There is an emotional component in all of our interpersonal dealings, and many experts say that while your cognitive intelligence often plays a stronger role in helping you get hired, it is your "emotional intelligence" that determines where you end up in your career. In general, emotional intelligence is simply your capacity to deal effectively with your own and others' emotions. In the workplace, it can determine how confident you are, how well you take the initiative, how effective a team player you are, and how well you handle conflicts.

In his new book *'Working with Emotional Intelligence'*, Goleman focuses on the need for emotional intelligence at work, an area often considered more head than heart. Not only do bosses and corporate leaders need high doses of emotional intelligence, but every people-oriented job demands it too, Goleman argues. Also, whereas IQ is relatively fixed, emotional intelligence can be built and learned, he claims. Companies can test and teach emotional intelligence, and many employers are already beginning to do so, he says.

However, while some psychologists view Goleman's proposition as an encouraging prescription for building career skills, others say its validity is as yet unproven. Some of the theory's critics question the way emotional intelligence is defined and claim it cannot be taught. Others maintain that cognitive and technical skills ultimately qualify people for the best jobs and help them excel at those jobs.

According to Dr. Goleman, recent research shows that emotions play an important part in who gets promoted and who gets fired. Of all the skills that distinguish leaders who reach the highest levels of corporations, the one that stands out is the ability to keep calm under pressure, says Dr. Goleman, who in his book "Primal Leadership" looks at how emotional intelligence affects leadership. The best leaders, he holds, are people who are comfortable with emotion.

Bosses and leaders, in particular, need high EQ because they represent the organisation to the public, they interact with the highest number of people within and outside the organisation and they set the tone for employee morale, says Goleman. Leaders with empathy are able to understand their employees' needs and provide them with constructive feedback, he says.

Different jobs also call for different types of emotional intelligence, Goleman says. For example, success in sales requires the empathic ability to gauge a customer's mood and the interpersonal skill to decide when to pitch a product and when to keep quiet. By comparison, success in painting or professional tennis requires a more individual form of self-discipline and motivation.

And there are gender differences in emotional intelligence as well, says Stein. After administering EQ assessments to 4,500 men and 3,200 women, his organisation found that women score higher than men on measures of empathy and social responsibility, but men outperform women on stress tolerance and self-confidence measures. In other words, says Stein, women and men are equally as intelligent emotionally, but they are strong in different areas.

Emotional Intelligence is Learned

Although children are born with different temperaments, or how they approach things—social, laid back, intense, shy, etc., EQ helps parents and teachers work with these qualities so children can better cope in the world. For example, instead of protecting shy children from the world and catering to them, parents encouraged their young children to participate in challenging situations (meeting new kids, going to new places). They encourage in ways that kids were not overwhelmed, but used methods that gave the children the experience of mastering something new. By the time these children reached kindergarten age, they were not shy. They were not the most outgoing children, but they were not the most withdrawn either.

The first step to increasing emotional intelligence is self-awareness. What are your feelings and why are you feeling that way? Although this can be very difficult for some, once a person begins to understand himself or herself, he or she can begin to develop other emotional skills, which leads to more emotional intelligence. *There are some patterns that block the use of a person's emotional intelligence: fear and worry, avoiding pain, negative self-image, unrealistic expectations, and blaming others. When these blocks occur and emotional intelligence is not used, people end up acting in unsuccessful ways. The goal is to be more informed about emotions and let them help overcome obstacles in life.*

Patterns of emotional intelligence are not fixed, however. So men and women can boost their all-round EQ by building their emotional abilities where they lack them, claims Stein. Working with psychologists and executive coaches, for example, women can hone their assertiveness skills and learn such stress-management techniques as meditation, yoga and jogging, says Stein. Men can learn the importance of listening to co-workers and customers, reading their moods and winning their trust—all increasingly important aspects of leadership, teamwork and customer and co-worker relations, says Stein.

Indeed, notes Goleman, the real value of the growing work on emotional intelligence is its implications for workplace training. 'IQ is relatively stable throughout life but much of emotional skill is learned,' says Goleman. He predicts that companies will increasingly opt for EQ training as they realise that it raises job productivity and customer satisfaction. His book explores models and guidelines for such training. 'Emotional intelligence affects just about everything you do at work,' says Goleman. 'Even when you work in a solitary setting, how well you work has a lot to do with how well you discipline and motivate yourself.'

Dr. Goleman says *anyone can learn to increase his or her emotional intelligence at any point. The quickest and most effective way, he says, is to get honest feedback from people around you and to develop a profile of your perceived strengths and weaknesses.* This strategy helped Peter Benton, 39, develop his leadership abilities and get assessments of his emotional intelligence. Working with a coach, he got his boss, several peers and a number of employees who reported to him to provide feedback. Although Mr. Benton recently left Johnson and Johnson, where he was a vice president, as a result of a restructuring, he says the coaching helped him develop a number of skills at his previous post, including maintaining calm under pressure. He knew he was on the right track, he says, when a subordinate came up to him one day and said, "I don't know what you're doing differently lately, but you're acting like a different person, and I feel we're more of a team."

❏❏❏

Chapter 16

Onion Model to Understand a Person

> *"When you meet someone better than yourself, turn your thoughts to becoming his equal. When you meet someone not as good as you are, look within and examine yourself."*
>
> **–Confucius**

We watch other people's behaviour-and are ourselves concerned with how we appear to others because that is all the data on which to build an understanding of another person. All the rest is inferred, not seen: what he means by what he says, what "he is after" , finally "the kind of person" he is. To infer correctly means analyzing and understanding better the apparent behaviour. Often we forget that outer behaviour, is like an outer crust which has more basic parts inside it. It is the same with understanding ourselves. We need to know what underlines our behaviour and what causes our behaviour.

Now the question is, how can we do that? We have to go inside step by step. We can imagine the self as an onion which has many layers. When we peel off the outer layer we get to a second, and on to the third, and so on. The outer layer is the layer of our external behaviour. When we peel off our feelings, we reveal our general attitudes. Below this are even more general values and our point of view. Embedded inside, a sort of kernel is our self concept, *i.e.,* the way we see ourselves. This, as we know well, is more stubborn phenomenon. Fair enough: our self concept is the compass of our lives; we steer by it. Yet true learning means clarifying and integrating further the picture we have of ourselves.

We can know the self only when we try to go deeper and look inside. It is not all easy to do so; the outer layer cannot be peeled off easily. Conditions can be fostered which help ensure, or at least encourage, the process of peeling to look inside. These we can label a climate of psychological safety. In a sense, only a bold attempt will do. Experiences like the one we are having in sensitivity sessions are best suited to peel off layer by layer in order to know the real self.

A start can be made by dealing with feelings. It may be necessary to ask yourself questions about your attitudes to the whole programme in order to know how best you can benefit from such an experience. You can ask yourself whether you have the attitude of a critical learner of "who cares", the attitude of "too old or too clever to learn" or of one who is curious and concerned about his own development and the development of the world around him. You can be the person to put such a question to yourself best of all.

Having examined your feelings you can also express them and so help others understand you. And so on through at least the first few layers of the onion. This task is never finished, of understanding oneself and expressing this so that others can understand you. It is the basis of living and working together of organisation, of personal satisfaction for most of us.

The same process can be applied to understand others. The first step in understanding a person is to note the feelings he expresses through his overt behaviour. The second is to see the uniformities of feelings and group them constellations. The last step is to relate these constellations and put them into a pattern or picture of the person. Diagrammatically these three steps can be expressed as show in Exhibit 16.1:

This self-concept, what we each think of ourselves, is the quietest part of us and also the most important. It is not affected much by daily events, which are to it what ripples on the surface of a body of water are to its

Exhibit 16.1: Understanding a Person

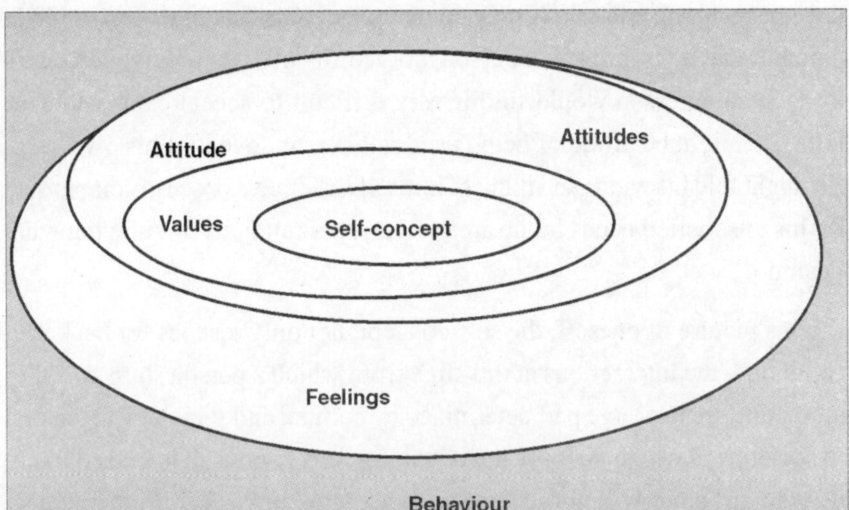

depth. Though developed through contact with other people, it is not oriented towards them, has no show, no seeming in it. It is how a person feels about himself deep down what manner of man he is, naked to his own self-knowledge. It is the level at which we all pursue lifelong quest;.' Who am I?" The other levels, one's points of view, his feelings and the way he behaves are all based on this last step, on his understanding of himself. In trying to understand a person properly, this is the level one has to listen for, it may never be stated, or it may not be at all clear land formulated to the person whose self-concept it is. This is the person's integrity which he will defend in order to survive as the person he understand himself to be. Any disintegration of personality, *e.g.,* by sickness or brain washing, is a disintegration (and perhaps reassembling differently) of a person's self-concept. The notion of personal worth is found here, the notion that I am not a person worthy of love and respect. The way it comes about can be described through an example; X is a fourth child, the second son of his family. He sees his parents and sisters pay much attention to the elder brother. He is envious of him. He may try to do many things to have some attention for himself. One would be to ingratiate himself by behaviour he knows to be approved; another to demand it by behaviour which will at least be noticed, like being naughty, breaking something and the like. This second is a slippery slope by which his very behaviour and attention: for naughty behaviour leads to a different tenuously more and more difficult. If this goes on long enough, X may conclude not only that others do not love him, but that he is unlovable person, not worthy of their or anybody else's love. Such a person would find it very difficult to accept expressions of love. He might be afraid of being used rather than loved for his own sake. He might fold his wings and think of himself as helpless or see to compensate for his unsatisfied needs in the area of personal relations by showing what I can do.

This picture of oneself, the self-concept, not only reaches for back into childhood, the interactions at this time from which a person starts forming his picture are to a large part determined by cultural and sociological factors. In societies in which girls are not equal in status to boys, it is indeed likely that the girl child will not receive as much attention as her brother and so learn not only that she is a person of secondary importance, but also one who is helpless and unable to take decisions. More fortuitous circumstances may lead a person to feel that he will succeed in whatever he tries and in less fortuitous circumstances another person may feel that he is "unlucky' and that the world is against him.

Some Examples of Building a Picture of a Person

The following chart follows through for the 'types' of people the kinds of observable behaviour and feelings in specific situations which characterise them. It goes on to indicate the directions in which they have most to learn.

Exhibit 16.2: Types of Self-Concept

Three Common types of self-Concept	***"Friendly Helper"***	***"Logical Thinker"***	***"Strong Doer"***
A. Observations are:			
Methods of influence	Doing favours Praising. Appealing. Being Entertaining. Appealing to pity.	Appeals to logic and facts. Shrewd argument. Appeals to rules and regulations, overwhelming knowing	Giving orders Giving a challenge, Threatening or Depriving

Three Common types of self-Concept	*"Friendly Helper"*	*"Logical Thinker"*	*"Strong Doer"*
Typical functions in group	Harmonising Tension Reduction Compromising Gate-keeping (by Concern) Expressing Warmth	Gathering information, Clarifying ideas and words Systematising Procedures Evaluating Proposals	Initiating Coordinating Discipline Exploring differences Gate-keeping (by Command Pressing for Results.
B. Feelings are:			
Mode of Evaluating	Who helps and likes people? Who hurts people?	Who is correct and accurate? Who is incorrect and mistaken?	Who is winning? Who is loosing?
Stress tends to Produce	Clinging dependence. Feeling of Depression.	Withdrawal Rigid adherence to rules and regulations	Domination Exploitation Overactivity impulsive action
Common fears	Loss of affection (Loneliness) Open conflict Attack	Confusion (loss of clarity and structure becoming obligated (indebtedness) being overwhelmed by Feeling or impulse.	Loss of power (illness or injury) becoming "softy" or "sentimentalist"
Emotional Style	Accepts in himself and in others love, affection, tender-ness, warmth, and	Rejects tough and tender emotions, Substitutes logic, accuracy, knowledge,	Accepts aggression, etc.Rejects affection, etc.

❐❐❐

Chapter 17

Eric Berne's Theory of Transactional Analysis

> *"One may understand the cosmos, but never the ego; the self is more distant than any star."*
> **–G. K. Chesterton**
> **(English born Gabonese Critic, Essayist, Novelist and Poet, 1874-1936)**

Transactional Analysis is a theory developed by Dr. Eric Berne in the 1950's. Originally trained in psychoanalysis, Berne wanted a theory which could be understood and available to everyone to understand human personality. Transactional Analysis theories outline how we treat ourselves, how we relate and communicate with others, and offer suggestions and interventions which will enable us to change and grow. Transactional Analysis is underpinned by the philosophy that people can change and we all have a right to be in the world and be accepted.

Roots of Transactional Analysis

Throughout history, and from all standpoints: philosophy, medical science, religion; people have believed that each man and woman has a multiple nature. In the early 20th century, Sigmund Freud first established that the human psyche is multi-faceted, and that each of us has warring factions in our subconscious. Since then, new theories continue to be put forward, all concentrating on the essential conviction that each one of us has parts of our personality which surface and affect our behaviour according to different circumstances.

In 1951, Dr. Wilder Penfield began a series of scientific experiments. Penfield used conscious human subjects and proved that by touching a part of the brain (the temporal cortex) with a weak electrical probe, the brain could be caused to 'play back' certain past experiences, and the feelings associated with them. The patients 'replayed' these events and their feelings despite not normally being able to recall them using their conventional memories.

Penfield's experiments went on over several years, and resulted in wide acceptance of the following conclusions:

- The human brain acts like a tape recorder, and whilst we may 'forget' experiences, the brain still has them recorded.
- Along with events the brain also records the associated feelings, and both feelings and events stay locked together.
- It is possible for a person to exist in two states simultaneously (because patients replaying hidden events and feelings could talk about them objectively at the same time).
- Hidden experiences when replayed are vivid, and affect how we feel at the time of replaying.
- There is a certain connection between mind and body, *i.e.,* the link between the biological and the psychological, *e.g.*, a psychological fear of spiders and a biological feeling of nausea.

Early Transactional Analysis Theory and Model

In the 1950 s, Eric Berne began to develop his theories of transactional analysis. He considered a *transaction* as the unit of social intercourse. A transaction consists of a transactional *stimulus (TS)* and a *transactional response (TR).* He said that verbal communication, particularly face to face, is at the centre of human social relationships and psychoanalysis. His starting-point was that when two people encounter each other, one of them will speak to the other. This he called the Transaction Stimulus. The reaction from the other person he called the Transaction Response. The person sending the Stimulus is called the *Agent.* The person who responds is called the *Respondent.* Various components of Transactional Analysis (TA) are:

- Structural Analysis
- Transactional Analysis
- Life position Analysis
- Games Analysis and
- Script Analysis

Structural Analysis

The process of analyzing personality in terms of ego states is called structural analysis. Berne devised the concept of ego states to help explain how we are made up, and how we relate to others. Berne also said that each person is made up of three alter ego states: *Parent, Adult and Child,* as shown in exhibit 8. These terms have different definitions than in normal language. They categorise the ways we think, feel and behave. When people interact they do so in one of three different ego states. An ego state is a specific way of thinking feeling and behaving and each ego state has its origin in specific regions of the brain.

In other words:

- Parent is our 'Taught' concept of life.
- Adult is our 'Thought' concept of life.
- Child is our 'Felt' concept of life.

People can behave from their Parent ego state, or from their Child ego state or from their Adult ego state. At any one time our actions come from one of these three ego states. Each ego state is further divided into sub-states based on their functions. Parent has *two functions (Controlling and Nurturing),* Adult has *one function (task)* and Child has *three functions (Natural (fun-loving, rebellious or impulsive), little professor (curios and creative) and adaptive.*

Exhibit 17.1: Structural Diagram of Ego States

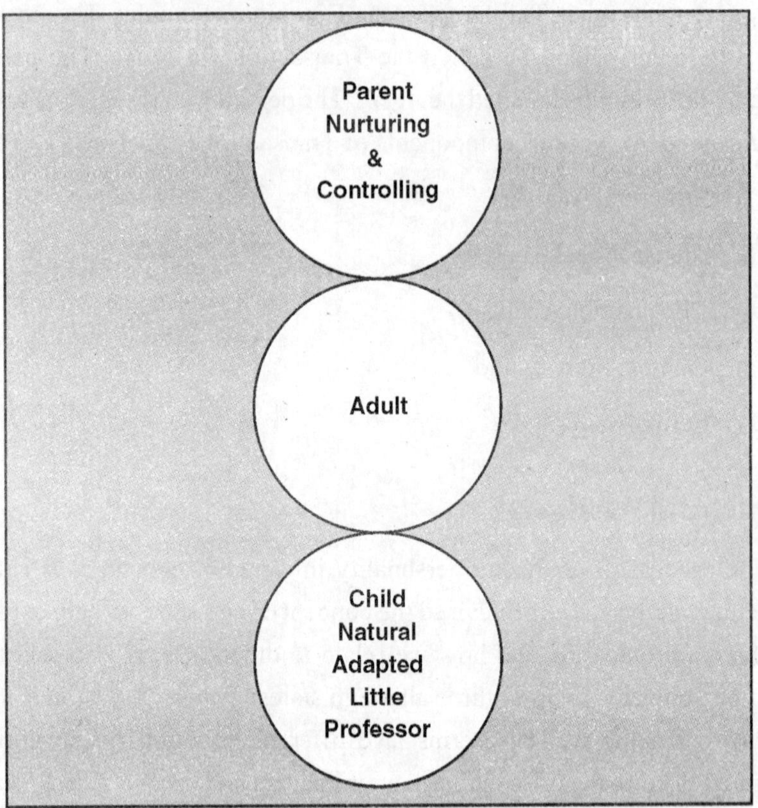

Parent Ego State

When a person is in the parent ego state she thinks, feels and behaves like one of her parents or someone who took their place. The parent decides, without reasoning, how to react to situations, what is good or bad, and how people should live. This is our ingrained voice of authority, absorbed conditioning, learning and attitudes from when we were young. This is also a set of feelings, thinking and behaviour that we have copied from our parents and significant others. We were conditioned by our real parents, teachers, older people, next door neighbours, aunts and uncles.

Our parent is made up of a huge number of hidden and overt recorded playbacks. The parent is like a tape recorder. It is a collection of pre-recorded, pre-judged, prejudiced codes for living. Typically embodied by phrases and attitudes starting with 'how to', 'under no circumstances', 'always', 'never forget', 'don't lie, cheat, steal', etc, etc. Our parent is formed by external events and influences upon us as we grow through early childhood. We can change it, but this is easier said than done. The parent judges for or against and can be controlling or supportive. There are two forms of parent we can play *Critical Parent and Nurturing Parent.*

- The *Nurturing Parent* is caring and concerned and often may appear as a mother-figure (though men can play it too). They seek to keep the Child safe and offer unconditional love, calming them when they are troubled. They are always reasonable, listen to other's opinions. Common phrases used are "you're great", "how can I support you", "how would you like to do that".

  The position in life is 'I'm ok you're ok.

Exhibit 17.2 : Nurturing Parent

Positive Qualities	***Negative Qualities***
I. Helpful, kind and encouraging.	1. Does too much for others (fusses over them).
2. Defender and protecter.	2. Overprotective.
3. Empathetic.	3. Smooths over problems. (instead of dealing with them).

- The *Controlling (or Critical) Parent*, on the other hand, tries to make the child do as the parent wants them to do, perhaps transferring values or beliefs or helping the child to understand and live in society. They may also have negative intent, using the child as a whipping-boy or worse. Common phrases used are "You must", "you should", and it is generally intolerant. The position in life is 'I'm ok you're not'. Common phrases used are "have you had dinner", "Where are you" etc.

  The position in life is 'I'm ok, you're not'.

Exhibit 17.3 : The Controlling (or Critical) Parent

Positive Qualities	*Negative Qualities*
1. Sets rules and standards	1. Inflexible.
2. Teaches and gives advice	2. Demands others do as he/she says
3. Makes decisions for others	3. Forces decisions on others.
4. Saves others when they are in trouble	4. Expects others to obey
5. Gives rewards	5. Gives punishm
6. Firm (strict)	6. Sometimes loud and angry

Child Ego State

The child ego state is a set of behaviours, thoughts and feelings which are replayed from our own childhood. When we are in the child ego state we act like the child we once were. We aren't just putting on an act; we think, feel, see, hear and react as a three or five or eight year old child. Perhaps the boss calls us into his or her office, we may immediately get a churning in our stomach and wonder what we have done wrong. If this were explored we might remember the time the head teacher called us in to tell us off.

In transactional analysis (TA) the child is seen as the source of creativity, recreation and procreation; the only source of renewal in life. The child can be observed in grownups in situations where people have permission to let the child out, like at sport events or parties. The child will appear for short periods of time in other situations, such as board meetings, classrooms or serious discussions where it may not be desired at all. In its most undesirable form it completely dominates a person's life, as in the cases of persons who are severely emotionally disturbed.

The child has all the feelings; fear, love, anger, joy, sadness, shame and so on. The child is often blamed for being the source of people's troubles because it is self-centered, emotional, and resists the suppression that comes with growing up.

It is divided further into two parts called sub ego-states, as given below:

- **Natural Child :** He has fun, loves nature, is spontaneous, sings, and dances, is usually inclusive of everybody, but can enjoy his/her own company and is not self-conscious. Common phrases used are "Wow", "lets", "Why don't we". The natural child is ready for fun without fear, shame or guilt. The position in life is 'I'm ok your ok'.

Exhibit 17.4 : Natural Child

Positive Qualities	*Negative Qualities*
1. Open (Disclose feelings).	1. Over-emotional.
2. Curious.	2. Nosy.
3. Has a sense of humor.	3. Joke around too much.
4. Take initiative.	4. Too impulsive.
5. Friendly and extroverted.	5. Selfish and noisy.
6. Fun to be with.	6. Considered naive and immature.

- **Adapted Child :** He/She is manipulative, self-centred and demanding. Often feels lost, alone, abandoned and unloved, is secretive and confused. Common phrases used are "its always my fault", "I have to", "mine is better than yours", "I should". The Positions in life is 'I'm not ok your not ok' or 'I'm not ok, you are ok'.

Exhibit 17.5 : Adapted Child

Positive Qualities	*Negative Qualities*
1 Polite and well-behaved.	1. Passive, lacks confidence.
2. Obedient and follows rules.	2. Follows rules without reason.
3. Helpful and cooperative.	3. Sometimes taken advantage of.
4. Keeps "place" in regard to age and sex.	4. Inflexible in understanding roles.

Adult Ego State

The adult ego state is about direct responses to the here and now. We deal with things that are going on today in ways that are not unhealthily influenced by our past. When in our adult we are able to see people as they are, rather than what we project onto them. We ask for information rather than making assumptions. When in the adult ego state the person functions as a human computer. It operates on data it collects and stores or uses to make decisions according to a logic-based program.

In the adult ego state the person uses logical thinking to solve problems making sure that child or parent emotions do not contaminate the process. People may conclude from this that emotions are not good. But it only means that in order to be rational and logical we need to be able to separate ourselves from our emotions. Being a mature human being or grownup is not the same as being in the adult ego state. Little children can be in their adult and well-adjusted grown-ups use their parent and child all the time.

The adult computes all the facts fed into it. If the facts are up-to-date, then the adult's answers will be timely and more effective than the parent's solution. If the facts are incorrect, the adult computer will produce incorrect answers. A very important function of the Adult is to predict outcomes and to provide a fact-based critique of the effectiveness of people's behaviour in the pursuit of their chosen goals. This fact-based, critical function is different from the value-based function of the Critical Parent.

Exhibit 17.6 : Adult Ego State

Positive Qualities	***Negative Qualities***
1. Logical, rational, objective and fair. 2. Cool and calm. 3. Assertive. 4. Good problem solver and decision maker. 5. Competent.	1. Too serious. 2. Cold and insensitive. 3. Annoying. 4. Ignores intuition and past experience. 5. Boring.

Sometimes the adult uses information which has its source in the child or in the parent and which may be incorrect. This is known as **contamination**. When a contamination comes from the parent it is called a *prejudice.* For instance when someone assumes that women prefer to follow a man's lead instead of making their own decisions this is data which comes to the adult from the parent, and is a contamination because it is accepted as a fact without checking it against reality.

The same unchecked acceptance of information can occur with information fed by the child in which case it is called *delusion.* A delusion is usually based on a child fear or hope that is accepted as reality by the Adult. For instance when a person is convinced that he is being poisoned by the government this is probably based on his child's fears which the Adult accepts, rather than on fact. An extremely important process in transactional analysis is decontamination of the adult.

Transactions: Complementary, Crossed and Covert

Transactions occur when any person relates to any other person. Each transaction is made up a stimulus and a response and transactions can proceed from the parent, adult or child of one person to the parent, adult or child of another person. A complimentary transaction involves same ego state in each person. In a crossed transaction the transactional response is addressed to an ego state different from the one which started the stimulus.

Berne identifies three types of transactions: *Complementary, Crossed and Covert.* Communication can continue between two people as long as transactions are *complimentary*. Problems usually occur in *Crossed* transactions, since the other person is at a different level. *Covert* transactions occur when people say one thing and mean another. Covert transactions are the basis of games and are especially interesting because they are deceptive. They have a social (overt) and a psychological (covert) level.

One important reason we say one thing and mean another is that we are generally ashamed of our child's or parent's desires and feelings. Nevertheless, we act on these desires and express those feelings while we pretend to be doing otherwise. For instance, we may use smiling sarcasm instead of a direct expression of our anger, or when scared we may counter-attack instead of admitting our fears. When we want attention or love we often feign indifference, and we have trouble giving or accepting them. In fact, because our lives are so immersed in half-truth and deception it can happen that we no longer know what it is our child really wants.

We also do not expect people to be completely honest, so we never really know whether we can trust what they say. Transactional analysts encourage people to be honest with one another, and with themselves, about their wants and feelings, rather than "crooked" and covert. In this manner people can find out what they want, how to ask for it and, if possible, how to get it.

Complementary Transactions

Complementary transactions are when a message gets the expected response from the other person. Communication proceeds smoothly as long as transactions are complementary. It occurs between two 'ego states' which reward one another. Though, Adult-to-Adult transactions are most effective, communication and understanding can occur in Parent-to-Child, Parent-to-Parent, or in Child-to-Child complementary transactions also.

Examples of Complementary Transactions: Parent-Parent, Adult-Adult, Child-Child, Child-Parent, Parent-Child, Child-Adult, Adult-Child, Adult-Parent, Parent-Adult

Example :

Student: *I am sorry that I did not complete my homework, but I was at the hospital all night long because my dad broke his leg and needed to go the ER.*

Teacher: *Thank you for explaining. We will work out another time for you to complete the assignment.*

The student from the Adult Ego State addresses the Teacher's Adult Ego State and the teacher responds from their Adult Ego State. Here the transactional vectors are parallel. The teacher and the student are complementing each others' conversation.

Crossed Transactions

When Transactional Stimulus (TS) and Transactional Receiver (TR) respond from different ego states, transactions are said to be crossed. Problems usually occur in Crossed transactions, since the other person is at a different level. The rule is "When TS and TR in the P-A-C diagram cross each other, communication stops."." The rule is: "whenever a disruption of communication occurs, a crossed transaction caused it Crossed transactions

Exhibit 17.7 : Complimentary Transactions

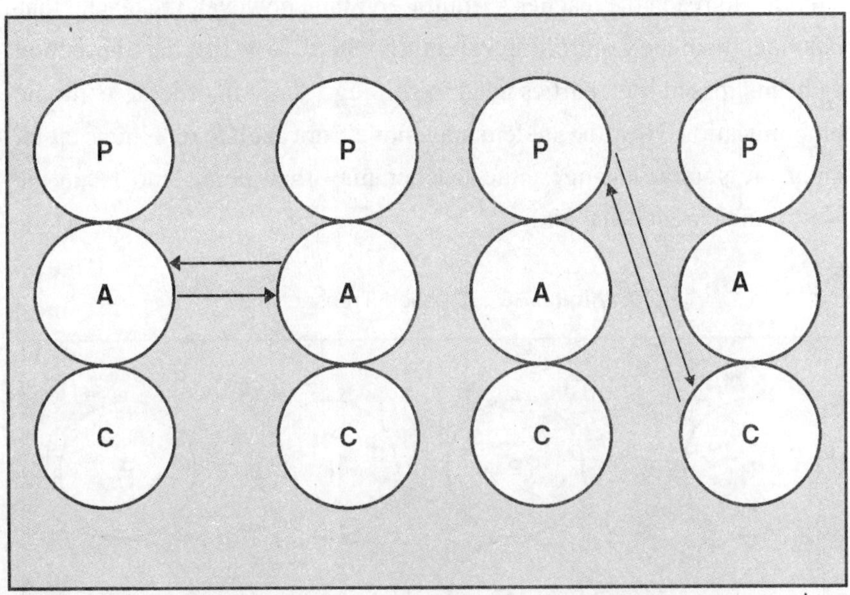

are important because it helps transactional analysts understand how and why communication is disrupted.

The parent is either nurturing or controlling, and often speaks to the child, who is either adaptive or 'natural' in their response. When both people talk as a Parent to the other's Child, their wires get crossed and conflict results. The ideal line of communication is the mature and rational Adult-Adult relationship.

Examples of Crossed Transactions: Adult-Adult and Parent-Child; Adult-Adult and Child-Parent; Parent-Child and Parent-Child; Child-Parent and Child-Parent

Example:

Student: *I am really sorry that I haven't finished my homework, but I was at the hospital all night long because my dad broke his leg and needed to go to the ER.*

Teacher: *I am not interested in your excuses, you know the rules. No homework, you get a zero for the assignment.*

As in the complementary transaction, the student is using their Adult Ego State to reach the teacher's Adult Ego State, however, the teacher has responded with the Controlling Parent Ego State. Now that the transaction has been crossed both parties need to shift ego states in order to continue communication. Now the student may move from adult to rebellious child. When the student changes, the teacher may then come into Negative Controlling Parent behavior.

Exhibit 17.8 : Crossed Transactions

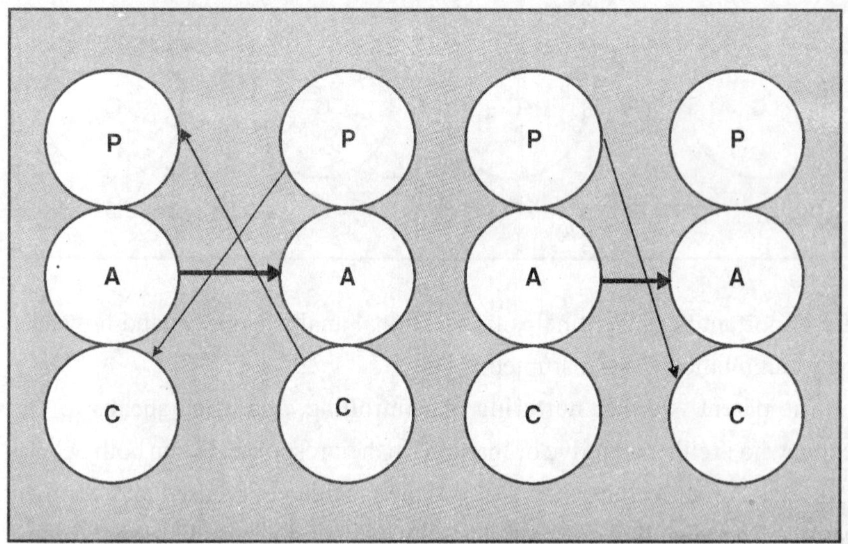

Ulterior Transactions

In an ulterior transaction there are actually two sub-transactions or messages, a social one and a psychological one. The psychological message is hidden and covert while the social message is overt and easily heard. Frequently with ulterior transactions, the social message is Adult to Adult but the psychological message is Parent to Child or Child to Parent. So two things are happening at the same time in an ulterior transaction; *first* is the words that are spoken and the meaning they convey, and *secondly* is the tone, gesture, posture, emphasis, and all other 'body language' with the implied meanings they convey.

Exhibit 17.9 : Ulterior Transactions

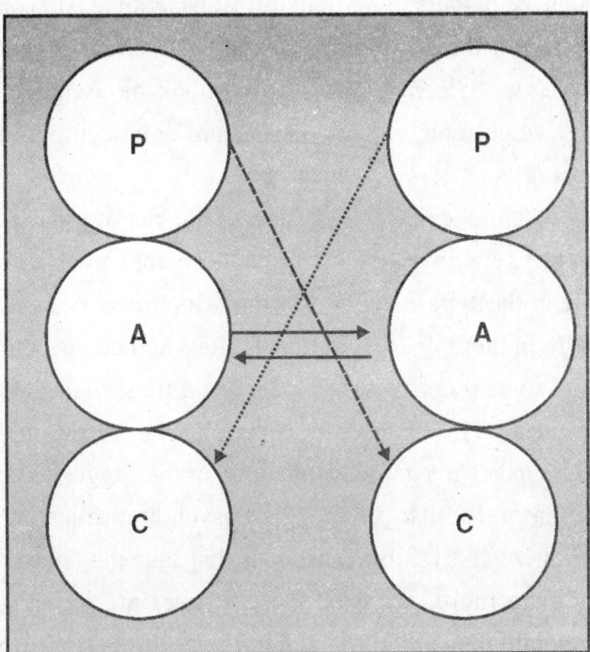

Examples of Crossed Transactions: Adult-Adult and Parent-Child; Adult-Adult and Child-Parent; Parent-Child and Parent-Child; Child-Parent and Child-Parent

Example:

Person A: *"What happened at the meeting yesterday?" (Question from adult to adult); whereas Ulterior Message is, "You should have given me a report before now."*

Person B: *There was a lot of discussion of the sales figures." (Answer from adult to adult); whereas Ulterior Message: "Your performance was criticised."*

Game Analysis

Berne defined certain socially dysfunctional behavioural patterns as "games." A ***game*** is a recurring series of covert transactions with a beginning, middle and end, and a ***payoff***. The payoff is a hidden advantage which motivates the players to participate. Transactional Analysis became a nation-wide fad in the 1960's due to the best selling success of Eric Berne's book, *Games People Play*. In this book he assigned engaging names ("Now I've got you," "Kick me," "I am only trying to help.") for different games.

For instance when Jane plays "Why don't You, Yes But" she asks advice from another but rejects every suggestion so that everyone ends up exasperated. It is the type of conversation which occurs over and over again, especially in therapy groups. It is devious and covert: on the social level, it appears to be a conversation between a person, in the Adult ego state, asking a question from one or more people who are also in their Adult ego states. What makes it a game is that none of the suggestions are really accepted. The reason for that is that, at the psychological and much more meaningful level, what is really going on is that Jane may need advise but needs strokes even more. Because these strokes are being given in a roundabout way and they are not as satisfying as direct strokes would be. This is why the game ends on a note of depressed frustration. There are a number of ***payoffs*** of each game. Every game pays off at three different levels:

(1) The **biological pay-off** of a game is strokes. Even though games end badly, all the players get a considerable number of strokes-both positive and negative-out of playing the game;

(2) The **social pay-off** of a game is **time-structuring**. That means people are able to fill time which otherwise might have been dull and depressing with an exciting activity;

(3) The **existential pay-off** of a game is the way in which the game confirms the existential position of each player.

Ways to Deal with Games

There are various ways to stop a game, including the use of different options than the one automatically used. We can:

- ❑ Cross the transaction by responding from a different ego state than the one stimulus is designed to hook.

- Pick up the ulterior rather than the social message, *e.g.*, when a person says "I can't do this, I'm useless". Rather than saying "let me do this for you" instead say "It sounds like you have a problem. What do you want me to do about it?" (said from the Adult ego state).
- The opening message to the game always entails a discount. There are further discounts at each stage of the game. By detecting discounts we can identify game invitations and defuse them with options. (A discount is when we minimize, maximize or ignore some aspect of a problem which would assist us in resolving it. Such as saying in a whiny voice "This is too difficult for me to do", so we automatically help them).
- Replace the game strokes. Loss of strokes to the Child ego state means a threat to survival. We get a great many strokes from games, even if they are negative. However, if we do not obtain sufficient positive strokes, or give ourselves positive strokes, we will go for quantity rather than quality of strokes and play games to get them. This loss of strokes is also a loss of excitement that the game has generated.

Another way to think about this is to consider the game role we or the other person is likely to take. One way to discover this is to ask the following questions:

1. What keeps happening over and over again?
2. How does it start?
3. What happens next?
4. And then what happens?
5. How does it end?
6. How do I feel after it ends? (John James, 1973)

In Transactional Analysis we call compliments and general ways of giving recognition ***strokes.*** This name came from research which indicated that babies require touching in order to survive and grow. It apparently makes no difference whether the touching induces pain or pleasure - it is still important. On the whole we prefer to receive negative strokes than no strokes at all, at least that way we know we exist and others know we exist.

Strokes are essential to a person's life. Without them, Berne said, the "spinal cord will shrivel up." It has been shown that a very young child needs actual physical strokes in order to remain alive. Adults can get by on fewer physical strokes as they learn to exchange verbal strokes; positive strokes like praise or expressions of appreciation, or negative strokes like negative judgments or put downs. Therefore, the exchange of strokes is one of the most important things that people do in their daily lives. For instance in the game of "Why Don't You; Yes But" a person's existential position is that "nothing ever works out" so that every time the game is played it reinforces that position and justifies further depression.

Games are always played with responsibility and interest by everyone involved in them. In order to maintain his or her existential position person will find people who will play the game with him/her. All the players' parts in the game are equally important and they all derive a pay-off from it as well. When they participate in the game they too believe it will end in failure. They want strokes as well but are not surprised when person rejects all advice and everyone is depressed or angry as a consequence proving that you can not really help people or that people do not want to be helped and justifying their bad feelings as a consequence.

Life Positions Analysis

Life positions are basic beliefs about self and others, which are used to justify decisions and behaviour. In the process of developing an identity people define for themselves, early in life, what the meaning of their life or existence is. Some people decide they are OK and are going to have a good life; but many others decide they are not OK and will fail in some way. That expectation based on a **decision** of how life will be is their ***existential position***. People can feel ***OK or not OK*** about themselves and others so that there are four main existential positions:

"I'm OK, you're OK," ***"I'm OK you're not OK," "I'm not OK you're OK" and finally, "I'm not OK you're not OK."***

"I'm OK - You're OK" is probably the best-known expression of the purpose of transactional analysis: to establish and reinforce the position that recognises the value and worth of every person. Transactional analysts regard people as basically "OK" and thus capable of change, growth, and healthy interactions.

These life positions are perceptions of the world. The reality is I am just I am and you are just you are, therefore how I view myself and others are just that "views" not fact. However, we tend to act as if they are a fact. Just like when somebody says "I can't do this, I'm useless" rather than "I don't know how to do this, will you show me?" The latter is staying with the fact that they do not yet know how to do it, whilst the former links being useless with not being able to do something.

Exhibit 17.10 : Life Positions

	I'm not OK	*I'm OK*
You're not OK	A Avoidance	B Bossing
You're OK	D Diffident	C Competent/confident/creative

There is also the way in which we view life itself. If we consider that there is something wrong with us, and that others are not to be trusted and are not OK either, then the world would be a scary place and we are likely to experience life as tough and believe we will only be all right if we keep alert and on the look out for danger and difficulties.

Script Analysis

Eric Berne proposed that dysfunctional behaviour is the result of self-limiting decisions made in childhood in the interest of survival. Such decisions culminate in what Berne called the "***life script***," the pre-conscious life plan that governs the way life is lived out. Changing the life script is the aim of transactional analysis psychotherapy. Replacing violent organisational or societal scripting with cooperative non-violent behaviour is the aim of other applications of transactional analysis.

Transactional analysts believe that most people are basically OK and in difficulty only because their parents (or other grownups and influential young people) have exposed them to powerful injunctions and attributions with long-term harmful effects. People, early in their lives come to the conclusion that their lives will unfold in a predictable way; short, long, healthy, unhealthy, happy, unhappy depressed or angry, successful or failed, active or passive. When the conclusion is that life will be bad or self-damaging this is seen as a life script.

When life is guided by a script there are always periods in which the person appears to be evading his or her unhappy fate. This seemingly normal period of the script, is called the **counter-script**. The counter-script is active when the person's unhappy life plan gives way to a happier period. This is, however, only temporary and invariably collapses, giving way to the original scripting. For an alcoholic, this may be a period of sobriety; for a depressed person with a suicide script it may be a brief period of happiness which inevitably ends when the script's injunctions take over.

It is possible to observe a person's script in brief sequences of behaviour called **min-scripts** which constantly mimic and reinforce the script. The fact is that everything that goes on in people's mental and emotional life is reflected in their behaviour. That is how by studying people's transactions, transactional analysts are able to understand the ways and reasons of people's behaviour and help them stop playing games, change their scripts and get the most out of life.

Rackets: One aspect of scripts is the existential payoff of games is the bad feelings which are accumulated and can eventually blow up and lead to an emotional disaster. Each game's existential payoff accumulates to eventually cause a predicted script outcome. Some people collect angry feelings that they will eventually justify a divorce. Others accumulate depressive feelings toward a suicide. The fact that they are creating situations which produce the negative feelings of their script choice is called their **emotional racket**.

❑❑❑

Chapter 18

Erikson's Psychosocial Development Theory

> *Personality is to a man what perfume is to a flower.*
> **–Charles M. Schwab**

Erik Erikson's psychosocial crisis life cycle model (eight stages) of human development is a very significant, highly regarded and meaningful concept. Life is a series of lessons and challenges which help us to grow. Erikson's wonderful theory helps to tell us why. The theory is helpful for child development and adults too.

Erik Erikson first published his eight stage theory of human development in his book "*Childhood and Society (1950).*" The chapter featuring the model was titled 'The Eight Ages of Man'. He expanded and refined his theory in later books and revisions, notably: Identity and the Life Cycle (1959); Insight and Responsibility (1964); The Life Cycle Completed: A Review (1982, revised 1996 by Joan Erikson); and Vital Involvement in Old Age (1989). Various terms are used to describe Erikson's model, for example *Erikson's bio-psychosocial theory, Erikson's human development cycle* or *life cycle,* and variations of these. All refer to the same eight stages psychosocial theory, it being Erikson's most distinct work and remarkable model.

The word 'psychosocial' is Erikson's term, effectively from the words psychological (mind) and social (relationships). Erikson believed that his psychosocial principle is genetically inevitable in shaping human development. It occurs in all people. He also referred to his theory as 'epigenesis' and the 'epigenetic principle', which signified the concept's relevance to evolution (past and future) and genetics.

Exhibit 18.1 : Erikson's Psychosocial Virtues or Strengths at Various Life Stages

Crisis including adaptive strength	*Basic and secondary virtue (and related strengths)*	*Life stage / relationships / issues*
1. *Trust* v. *Mistrust*	Hope and Drive (faith, inner calm, grounding, basic feeling that everything will be okay-enabling exposure to risk, a trust in life and self and others, inner resolve and strength in the face of uncertainty and risk).	Infant / mother / feeding and being comforted, teething, sleeping.
2. *Autonomy* v. *Shame and Doubt*	Willpower and Self-Control (self-determination, self-belief, self-reliance, confidence in self to decide things, having a voice, being one's own person, persistence, self-discipline, independence of thought, responsibility, judgement).	Toddler / parents / bodily functions, toilet training, muscular control, walking.
3. *Initiative* v. *Guilt*	Purpose and Direction (sense of purpose, decision-making, working with and leading others, initiating projects and ideas, courage to instigate, ability to define personal direction and aims and goals, able to take initiative and appropriate risks)	Preschool / family / exploration and discovery, adventure and play.
4. *Industry* v. *Inferiority*	Competence and Method (making things, producing results, applying skills and processes productively, feelingvalued and capable of contributing, ability to apply method and process in pursuit of ideas or objectives, confidence to seek and respond to challenge and learning, active busy productive outlook)	Schoolchild/school, teachers, friends, neighbourhood / achievement and accomplishment.

Table Cont...

5. *Identity* v. *Role Confusion*	Fidelity and Devotion (self-confidence and self-esteem necessary to freely associate with people and ideas based on merit, loyalty, social and interpersonal integrity, discretion, personal standards and dignity, pride and personal identity, seeing useful personal role(s) and purpose(s) in life).	adolescent / peers, groups, influences / resolving identity and direction, becoming a grown-up.
6. *Intimacy* v. *Isolation*	Love and Affiliation (capacity to give and receive love - emotionally and physically, connectivity with others, socially and inter-personally comfortable, ability to form honest reciprocating relationships and friendships, capacity to bond and commit with others for mutual satisfaction - for work and personal life, reciprocity - give and take - towards good).	young adult / lovers, friends, work connections / intimate relationships, work and social life.
7. *Generativity* v. *Stagnation*	Care and Production (giving unconditionally in support of children and/or for others, community, society and the wider world where possible and applicable, altruism, contributing for the greater good, making a positive difference, building a good legacy, helping others through their own crisis stages.	Mid-adult / children, community / 'giving back', helping, contributing.
8. *Integrity* v. *Despair*	Wisdom and Renunciation (calmness, tolerance, appropriate emotional detachment - non-projection, no regrets, peace of mind, non-judgemental, spiritual or universal reconciliation, acceptance of inevitably departing).	Late adult / society, the world, life / meaning and purpose, life achievements, acceptance.

Erikson was careful to choose words for the maladaptations and malignancies which convey a lot of meaning and are very symbolic of the emotional outcomes that are relevant to each stage.

In each case the maladaptation or malignancy corresponds to an extreme extension of the relevant crisis disposition (for example, 'Withdrawal' results from an extreme extension of 'Mistrust'). Thinking about this helps to understand what these outcomes entail, and interestingly helps to identify the traits in people - or oneself - when you encounter the behavioural tendency concerned.

Malignancies and maladaptations can manifest in various ways. Here are examples, using more modern and common language, to help understand and interpret the meaning and possible attitudes, tendencies, behaviours, etc., within the various malignancies and malapdations. In each case the examples can manifest as more extreme mental difficulties, in which case the terms would be more extreme too. These examples are open to additional interpretation and are intended to be a guide, not scientific certainties. Neither do these examples suggest that anyone experiencing any of these behavioural tendencies is suffering from mental problems. Erikson never established any absolute measurement of emotional difficulty or tendency as to be defined as a malignancy or maladaptation.

In truth each of us is subject to emotional feelings and extremes of various sorts, and it is always a matter of opinion as to what actually constitutes a problem. All people possess a degree of maladaptation or malignancy from each crisis experience. Not to do so would not be human, since none of us is perfect. It's always a question of degree. It's also a matter of understanding our weaknesses, maybe understanding where they come from too, and thereby better understanding how we might become stronger, more productive and happier.

Freud's Psychosexual and Eriksson's Psychosocial Stages-Overview

Freud, like Erikson, was largely concerned with how personality and behaviour is influenced after birth and not before birth – and especially during childhood. In the *'nature v. nurture' (genes v. experience')* debate, Erikson was firmly focused on nurture and experience. Below is given an overview of Freud's psychosexual stages and its similarity with Erikson's psychosocial stages. Age guide is a broad approximation, hence the overlaps. The stages happen in this sequence, but not to a fixed timetable.

Exhibit 18.2 : Freud's Psychosexual and Erikson's Psychosocial Stages

Freud's psychosexual stages	***Erikson's psychosocial crisis stages***	***Age guide***
1. *Oral Stage :* Feeding, crying, teething, biting, thumb-sucking, weaning - the mouth and the breast are the centre of all experience. The infant's actual experiences and attachments to mum (or maternal equivalent) through this stage have a fundamental effect on the unconscious mind and thereby on deeply rooted feelings, which along with the next two stages affect all sorts of behaviours and (sexually powered) drives and aims - Freud's *'libido'* - and preferences in later life.	1. *Trust* v. *Mistrust*	0-1½ yrs, baby, birth to walking
2. *Anal Stage :* It's a lot to do with pooh - 'holding on' or 'letting go' - the pleasure and control. Is it dirty? Is it okay? Bodily expulsions are the centre of the world, and the pivot around which early character is formed. Am I pleasing my mum and dad? Are they making me feel good or bad about my bottom? Am I okay or naughty? Again the young child's actual experiences through this stage have a deep effect on the unconscious and behaviours and preferences in later life.	2. *Autonomy* v. *Shame and Doubt*	1-3 yrs, toddler, toilet training

Freud's psychosexual stages	*Erikson's psychosocial crisis stages*	*Age guide*
3. *Phallic Stage :* Phallic is not restricted to boys. This stage is focused on resolving reproductive issues. This is a sort of dry run before the real game starts in adolescence. Where do babies come from? Can I have a baby? Why has dad got a willy and I've not? Why have I got a willy and mum hasn't? Why do they tell me off for touching my bits and pieces down there? (Boys) I'm going to marry mum (and may be kill dad). (Girls) I'm in love with my dad. Oedipus Complex, Penis envy, Castration Anxiety, etc. "If you touch yourself down there it'll fall off/heal up..." Inevitably once more, experiences in this stage have a profound effect on feelings and behaviour and *libido* in later life.	3. *Initiative* v. *Guilt*	3-6 yrs, pre-school, nursery
4. *Latency Stage :* Sexual dormancy or repression. The focus is on learning, skills, schoolwork. This is actually not a psychosexual stage because basically normally nothing formative happens sexually. Experiences, fears and conditioning from the previous stages have already shaped many of the child's feelings and attitudes and these will re-surface in the next stage.	4. *Industry* v. *Inferiority*	5-12 yrs, early *school.*

Freud's psychosexual stages	Erikson's psychosocial crisis stages	Age guide
5. *Genital Stage :* Puberty in other words. Glandular, hormonal, and physical changes in the adolescent child's body cause a resurgence of sexual thoughts, feelings and behaviours. Boys start treating their mothers like woman-servant and challenge their fathers (Freud's 'Oedipus'). Girls flirt with their fathers and argue with their mums (Freud's 'Electra'). All become highly agitated if away from a mirror for more than half an hour (Freud's Narcissus or Narcissism). Dating and fondling quickly push schoolwork and sports (and anything else encouraged by parents and figures of authority) into second place. Basically everyone is in turmoil and it's mostly to do with growing up, which entails more sexual undercurrents than parents would ever believe, even though these same parents went through exactly the same struggles themselves just a few years before. It's a wonder anyone ever makes it to adulthood, but of course they do, and mostly it's all perfectly normal. This is the final Freudian psychosexual stage. Erikson's model, which from the start offers a different and more socially oriented perspective, continues through to old	5. *Identity* v. *Role Confusion*	11-18 yrs, puberty, teens earlier for girls.

Freud's psychosexual stages	*Erikson's psychosocial crisis stages*	*Age guide*
age, and re-interprets Freudian sexual theory into the adult life stages equating to Erikson's crisis stages. This incorporation of Freudian sexual stages into the adult crisis stages is not especially significant.		
6. Arguably no direct equivalent to Freudian stage, although as from Identity and the Life Cycle (1969) Erikson clearly separated Puberty and Genitality (Freud's Genital stage), and related each respectively to *Identity* v *Role Confusion*, and *Intimacy* v *Isolation*.	6. *Intimacy* v. *Isolation*	18-40, courting, early parenthood.
7. No direct equivalent Freudian stage, although Erikson later interpreted this as being a psychosexual stage of 'Procreativity'.	7. *Generativity* v. *Stagnation*.	30-65, middle age, parenting.
8. Again no direct equivalent Freudian stage. Erikson later called this the psychosexual stage of 'Generalisation of Sensual Modes'.	8. *Integrity* v. *Despair*	50+, old age, grandparents.

In Conclusion

Erikson's psychosocial theory is very powerful for self-awareness and improvement, and for teaching and helping others.

While Erikson's model emphasises the sequential significance of the eight character-forming crisis stages, the concept also asserts that humans continue to change and develop throughout their lives, and that personality is not exclusively formed during early childhood years. This is a helpful and optimistic idea, and many believe it is realistic too. It is certainly a view that greatly assists encouraging oneself and others to see the future as an opportunity for positive change and development, instead of looking back with blame and regret.

The better that people come through each crisis, the better they will tend to deal with what lies ahead, but this is not to say that all is lost and never to be recovered if a person has had a negative experience during any particular crisis stage. Lessons can be revisited successfully when they recur, if we recognise and welcome them.

Everyone can change and grow, no matter what has gone before. And as ever, understanding why we are like we are - gaining meaningful self-awareness - is always a useful and important step forward. Erikson's theory helps to enable this meaningful understanding and personal growth.

Erikson's psychosocial theory should be taught to everyone - especially to school children, teachers and parents - it's certainly accessible enough, and would greatly assist all people of all ages to understand the connections between life experiences and human behaviour - and particularly how grown-ups can help rather than hinder children's development into rounded emotionally mature people.

Erikson was keen to improve the way children and young people are taught and nurtured, and it would be appropriate for his ideas to be more widely known and used in day-to-day life, beyond the clinical and counselling professions.

Chapter 19

Neuro Linguistic Programming

> *"The only normal people are the one's you don't know very well."*
>
> **–Joe Ancis**

Neuro-Linguistic Programming (NLP) was created in the early 1970s by Richard Bandler, a computer scientist and Gestalt therapist, and Dr. John Grinder, a linguist and therapist. Bandler and Grinder invented a process known as 'Modelling' that enabled them to study three of the world's greatest therapists: Dr Milton Erickson, father of modern hypnotherapy; Fritz Perls, creator of Gestalt therapy; and Virginia Satir, the mother of modern-day family therapy. They wanted to know what made these therapists effective and to train others in their methods. What is offered today as NLP is the product of this Modelling process.

Neuro-Linguistic Programming is an extremely powerful concept. It is said to contain all the positive and the most useful aspects of modern psychology. The experience of undergoing NLP training is a life-changing one for many people, and its techniques offer substantial advantage to most roles in organisations:

NLP Operational Principles

NLP consists of a set of powerful techniques for rapid and effective behavioural modification, and an operational philosophy to guide their use. It is based on four operational principles:

1. *Know* what outcome you want to achieve.
2. Have sufficient *sensory acuity* (acuity means clear understanding) to know if you are moving towards or away from your outcome.
3. Have sufficient *flexibility of behaviour* so that you can vary your behaviour until you get your outcome.
4. Take *action* now.

This variation in behaviour is not random. It involves the systematic application of NLP patterns. It is also important to take action, since nothing ever happens until someone takes the initiative. In short, NLP is about *thinking, observing and doing* to get what you want out of life.

NLP Principle 1 : Achieving Outcomes

The importance of knowing your outcome cannot be stressed enough. Many people do not have conscious outcomes. Others have no idea what they want but know what they do not want. Their life is based on moving away from those things they do not want. NLP stresses the importance of *moving towards those things you want.* Without outcomes life becomes a process of wandering aimlessly. Once an outcome is determined you can begin to focus on achieving that outcome.

NLP lists certain *well-formed conditions* that outcomes should meet. The first of these is that the outcome needs to be *stated in positive terms*. This means that the outcome must be what you want and not what you do not want. Outcomes must be capable of being satisfied. It is both logically and practically impossible to give someone the negation of an experience. You can not engage in the process of 'not doing'. You can only engage in the process of doing.

The second well-formed condition for outcomes is that the outcome must be *testable and demonstrable in sensory experience*. There must be an evidence procedure. Unless this is the case, there is no way to measure progress towards the achievement of the outcome. With an evidence procedure for the outcome it is possible to determine whether or not you are making progress towards achieving the outcome.

Third, the desired state must be *sensory specific*. You must be able to say what you would look like, sound like and feel like if you achieved the outcome.

Fourth, the outcome or desired state must be *initiated and maintained by the subject*. This places the locus (*i.e.,* position) of control and responsibility for achieving the outcome with the subject and not with someone else. It is not a well-formed outcome when someone else does something or changes in some way. All you can do is have an outcome in which you can change yourself or your behaviour so as to bring about a change in someone else.

Fifth, the outcome must be *appropriately and explicitly contextualised*. This means that outcomes must not be stated as universals. You must never want either 'all the time' of 'never', but only under specific circumstances. In NLP we always strive to create more choice and never to take choice or reduce the number of possible responses. The goal instead is to make the choices or responses available in the appropriate circumstances.

Sixth, the desired outcome *must preserve any positive product of the present state*. If this is not the case then symptom substitution may occur.

Seventh and finally, the outcome or desired state must be *ecologically sound*. You should consider the consequences for yourself and for other people and not pursue outcomes that lead to harm to yourself or other people.

NLP Principle 2 : Sensory Awareness

Once you know your outcome you must next have sufficient sensory insight to know if you are moving towards it or not. NLP teaches the ability to calibrate or 'read' people. This involves the ability to interpret changes in muscle tone, skin colour and shininess, lower lip size and breathing rate and location. The NLP practitioner uses these and other indications to determine what effect they are having on other people. This information serves as feedback as to whether the other person is in the desired state. An important and often overlooked point is to know to stop when the other person is in the state that you desire.

NLP Principle 3 : Changing Behaviour

The third operational principle of NLP is to vary your behaviour until you get the response you want. If what you are doing is not working, then you need to do something else. You should use your sensory acuity to determine if what you are doing is leading you in the desired direction of not. It what you are doing is leading towards your outcome, then you should continue. If, on the other hand, what you are doing is leading away from your goals, then you should do something else.

NLP Principle 4 : Time for Action

The fourth and final operational principle of NLP is to take action now. In using any of these patterns NLP stresses the importance of continuous calibration of the person or people you are interacting with in order to see if what you are doing is working. If it is not working it is important to do something different. The idea is to *vary your behaviour until you get the results you want.* It is important to have specific outcomes.

There is no place for the slogan 'Complacency rules and I don't care.' NLP is about taking action now to change behaviour for yourself and for others, now and in the future. So, to use another catchphrase: 'Don't delay; act today.'

NLP Presuppositions

There are certain presuppositions underlying NLP. These are things that are presupposed in effective communication. Some of these are as follows:

NLP Presupposition 1 : Meaning Equals Response

The *meaning of a communication is the response* you get. In communication it is usually assumed that you are transferring information to another person. You have information that 'means' something to the other person and you intend for the other person to understand what it is you intended Meaning Equals Response to communicate. Frequently a person assumes that if they 'say what they mean to say', their responsibility for the communication is over. Effective communicators realise that their responsibility does not end when they finish talking. They realise that, for practical purposes, what they communicate is what the other person thinks they say and not what they intend to say. Often the two are quite different.

In communication it is important what the other person thinks you say and how they respond. This requires that the person pays attention to the response they are getting. If it is not the response they want, then they need to vary their own communication until they get the desired response.

There are several major sources of 'misunderstanding' in communication. The first arises from the fact that each person has a different life experience associated with each word in the language. Frequently, what one person means by a word may be something different from what another person means by it. The second misunderstanding arises from the failure to realise that a person's tone of voice and facial expression also communicate information, and that the other person may respond to these as much as they do to what is said. As the old saying goes, 'Actions speak louder than words'; in NLP people are trained that when the two are in conflict, the person should pay *more attention to the actions*.

NLP Presupposition 2 : The Map is not the Territory

Good communicators realise that the representations they use to organise their experience of the world ('map') are not the world ('territory').

It is important to distinguish between several semantic levels. *First there is the world. Second comes the person's experience of the world.* This experience is the person's 'map' or 'model' of the world and is different for each person. Every individual creates a unique model of the world and thus lives in a somewhat different reality from everyone else. You do not operate directly on the world but on your experience of it. This experience may or may not be correct. To the extent that your experience has a similar structure to the world it is correct and this accounts for its usefulness.

A person's experience, map, model or representation of the world determines how they will perceive the world and what choices they will see as available to them. Many NLP techniques involve you changing your representation of the world to make it more useful and to bring it more into line with the way the world actually is.

NLP Presupposition 3 : Language and Experience

Language is a secondary representation of experience. Language is at a third semantic level. *First is the stimulus coming from the world. Second is the person's representation of experience of that stimulus. Third is the person's description of that experience by way of language.* Language is not experience but a representation of it. Words are merely arbitrary tokens used to represent things the person sees, hears or feels. People who speak other languages use different words to represent the same things that English speakers see, hear or feel. Also, since each person has a unique set of things that they have seen, heard and felt in their lives, their words have different meanings from each of them.

People are able to communicate effectively to the degree that these meanings are similar. When they are too dissimilar, problems in communication begin to arise.

NLP Presupposition 4 : Body and Mind Affect Each Other

Mind and body are parts of the same cybernetic system and affect each other. There is no separate 'mind' and no separate 'body'. Both words refer to aspects of the same 'whole' or 'gestalt', they act as one and they influence each other in such a way that there is no separation.

Anything that happens in one part of a cybernetic system, such as a human being, will affect all other parts of that system. *This means that the way a person thinks affects how they feel and that the condition of their physical body affects how they think.* A person's perceptual input, internal thought process, emotional process, physiological response and behavioural output all occur both simultaneously and through time.

In practical terms, this means that a *person can change how they think either by directly changing how they think or by changing their physiology or other feelings.* Likewise, a person can change their physiology or their emotions by changing how they think. One important corollary of this, which will be explored later, is the importance of visualisation and mental rehearsal in improving the conduct of any activity.

NLP Presupposition 5 : The Law of Requisite Variety (also Known as the First Law of Cybernetic)

Cybernetics is the science of systems and controls in animals, (including humans, and machines) states that in any cybernetic system the element or person in the system with the widest range of behaviours or variability of choice will control the system. *Control in human systems refers to the ability to influence the quality of a person's own and other people's experience in the moment and through time.*

The person with the greatest flexibility of behaviour - that is, the number of ways of interacting - will control the system. Choice is always preferable to no choice, and more choice is always preferable to less choice. This also relates to the third general principle of NLP, mentioned previously. This principle is that a person needs to vary their behaviour until they get their desired outcome. If what you are doing is not working, vary the behaviour and do something else. Anything else is better than continuing with what does not work. Keep varying your behaviour until you find something that works.

NLP Presupposition 6 : Behaviour and Adaptation

Behaviour is geared towards adaptation. A person's behaviour is determined by the context in which that behaviour originates.

Your reality is defined by your perceptions of the world. The behaviour a person exhibits is appropriate to their reality. All of a person's behaviour, whether good or bad, is an adaptation. Everything is useful in some context. All behaviour is or was adaptive, given the context in which it was learned. In another context it may not be appropriate. People need to realise this and change their behaviour when it is appropriate to do so.

NLP Presupposition 7 : Best Choice of Behaviour

Behind every behaviour is a positive intent. A person makes the best choice available him/her at any moment at that time, based on all their life experiences and the choices they are aware of. If offered a better choice they will take it.

In order to change someone's inappropriate behaviour it is necessary to give them other choices. Once this is done they will behave accordingly. NLP has techniques for providing these additional choices. Also, in NLP we never take away choices. We only provide more choices and explicitly contextualise the existing choices.

NLP Presupposition 8 : Context of Behaviour

Present behaviour represents the very best choice available to a person. You need to evaluate your behaviour in terms of what you are capable of becoming. You need to strive to become all that you are capable of being.

NLP Presupposition 9 : Resources Needed to Change Behaviour

Behaviour is to be evaluated and appreciated or changed as appropriate in the context presented. People have all the resources they need to make the changes they want. The task is to locate or access those resources and to make them available in the appropriate context. NLP provides techniques to accomplish this task.

What this means in practice is that *people do not need to spend time trying to gain insight into their problems or in developing resources to deal with their problems.* They already have all the resources they need to deal with their problems. All that is necessary is to access these resources and transfer them to the current time frame.

NLP Presupposition 10 : The How of Possibility

'Possible in the world' or 'possible for me' is only a matter of how. If any other human being is capable of performing some behaviour, then it is possible for you to perform it, too. The process of determining 'how' you do it is called 'modelling', and it is the process by which NLP came into being in the first place.

NLP Presupposition 11 : Rely on the Behaviour rather than Words

The highest quality information about other people is behavioural. *Behaviour Speaks Louder than Words* Listen to what people say but pay more attention to what they do. If there is any contradiction between the two then rely on the behaviour. Look for behavioural evidence of change and don't just reply on people's words.

NLP Presupposition 12 : Distinguish Behaviour and Self

It is useful to make a *distinction between behaviour and self.* In other words, just because someone 'screws up' on something it does not mean that they are a 'screw-up'. Behaviour is what a person says, does or feels at any moment in time. This is not a person's self, however. *A person's self is greater than their behaviours.*

NLP Presupposition 13 : Feedback, Not Failure

There is no such thing as failure; there is only feedback. *It is more valuable for a person to view their experience in terms of a learning frame than in terms of a failure frame.* If a person does not succeed in something, that does not mean they have failed. It just means that they have discovered one way not to do that particular thing. The person then needs to vary their behaviour until they find a way to succeed.

Further Reading and References

1. Baumeister, R. F., & Bushman, B. J. (2008); *Social psychology and human nature* (1st ed.) Belmont, CA: Thomson Wadsworth.
2. Berne, Eric (1975); *A Layman's Guide to Psychiatry and Psychoanalysis (Paperback);* Grover Press.
3. Berne, Eric (1975); *What Do You Say After You Say Hello.*
4. Berne, Eric ; *Transactional Analysis in Psychotherapy,*(1996) (Paperback reissue ed.) New York: Ballantine Books.
5. Berne, Eric; *The Structure and Dynamics of Organizations and Groups.*
6. Eric Berne (1964); *Games People Play,* New York: Grove Press.
7. Bion, W.R. (1961); *Experiences in Groups*, London: Tavistock Publications.
8. Bogdan, R. C. and Biklen, S. K. (1992); *Qualitative Research for Education,* Boston: Allyn and Bacon.
9. Bradford, L. P., Gibb, J. R., Benn, K. D. (1964). *T Group theory and laboratory method,* New York: John Wiley.
10. Brown, R. (1988); *Group Processes: Dynamics within and between groups,* Oxford, Blackwell.
11. Carr, W. and Kemmis, S. (1986*): Becoming Critical. Education, knowledge and action research,* Lewes: Falmer Press.
12. Corkille Briggs, Dorothy (1986); *Celebrate Yourself*, Bantam Doubleday Dell Publishing Group.
13. Davidson, P, Griffin, RW. (2006); *Management;* Milton; John Wiley and Sons Australia LTD.
14. Dyer, William (1994); *Team Building,* 3rd Edition, Prentice Hall.
15. Elliott, J. (1991); *Action Research for Educational Change*, Buckingham: Open University Press.

16. Follett, M.P. (1925); *The giving of orders*, In J.M.Shafritz and J.S.Ott (eds) Classics of Organization Theory (4th ed) New York: Harcourt Brace College Publishers.

17. Forsyth, D.R. 2006; *Group Dynamics*, 4th Edition Belmont, CA: Thomson Wadsworth.

18. Freud, S. (1922);*Group Psychology and the Analysis of the Ego*; New York: Liveright Publishing.

19. Gastil, J. (1994); *A definition and illustration of democratic leadership' Human Relations* Reprinted in K. Grint (ed.) (1997) Leadership, Oxford: Oxford University Press.

20. Gold, M. (ed.) (1999); *The Complete Social Scientist*. A Kurt Lewin Reader.

21. Hall, C.S. and Lindzey, G. (1978); *Theories of Personality* 3e, New York: John Wiley and Sons.

22. Homans, G. C. (1974); *Social Behaviour: Its Elementary Forms*, Rev. Ed. New York, Harcourt Brace Jovanovich. ISBN 0-15-581417-6.

23. Ian Stewart, Vann Joines ; *TA Today: A New Introduction to Transactional Analysis (*1990) (Paperback reissue ed.)

24. Jones, John. E. (1973); *A model of group development*." Pfeiffer, J. William, and Jones, John E. (eds.), 1973 Annual Handbook for Group Facilitators, University Associates: La Jolla, CA.

25. Kariel, H. S: (1956) *'Democracy unlimited. Kurt Lewin's field theory'*, American Journal of Sociology 62: 280-89.

26. Klein, M. (1959) Our adult world and its roots in infancy. Human Relations 12 (4) 291-304. Reprinted in Colman, A. & Geller, M (1985) Group Relations Reader 2. Jupiter, FL: A.K.Rice Institute.

27. Kolb, D. A. (1984*): Experiential Learning: Experience as the source of learning and development,* Englewood Cliffs, NJ.: Prentice-Hall.

28. Le Bon, G. (1896); *The Crowd: A Study of the Popular Mind*, London: Ernest Benn Limited.

29. Lui and Chan (2008); *Software Development Rhythms*, John Wiley and Sons.

30. Lewin, K. (1935); *A dynamic theory of personality*. New York: McGraw-Hill.

31. Lewin, K. (1936*); Principles of topological psychology*, New York: McGraw-Hill.

32. Lewin, K. (1948): *Resolving social conflicts; selected papers on group dynamics.* Gertrude W. Lewin (ed.). New York: Harper & Row, 1948.

33. Lewin, K. (1951): *Field theory in social science;* selected theoretical papers. D. Cartwright (ed.). New York: Harper & Row.

34. Lewin, K. and Lippitt, R. (1938): *An experimental approach to the study of autocracy and democracy. A preliminary note'*, Sociometry 1: 292-300.

35. Lewin, K., Lippitt, R. and White, R. (1939): *Patterns of aggressive behaviour in experimentally created "social climates"'*, Journal of Social Psychology 10: 271-99.

36. Lewin, K. and Grabbe, P. (1945): *Conduct, knowledge and acceptance of new values'* Journal of Social Issues 2.

37. Lewin,K; (c 1951, APA Reprint 1997): *Field theory in social science*

38. Lippitt, R. (1949): *Training in Community Relations,* New York: Harper and Row.

39. Marrow, A. J. (1969); *The Practical Theorist. : The Life and Work of Kurt* Lewin, New York: Basic Books.

40. Mihaly Csikszentmihalyi; *Flow: The psychology of optimum experience.* (Harper and Row, 1991)

41. Mayo, E. (1933*) The Human Problems of an Industrialised Civilisation.* New York: Viking Press.

42. McDougall, W. (1920*) The Group Mind.* New York: G.P.Putnam.

43. Miller, E. (1989); *The Leicester Model: Experiential study of group and organizational processes.* (Tavistock Institute Occasional Paper No.10). London: Tavistock Institute of Human Relations.

44. Muriel James and Dorothy Jongeward; *Born to Win: Transactional Analysis with Gestalt Experiments* (Addison-Wesley, 1971)

45. Peck, M.S. (1987); *The Different Drum: Community-Making and Peace*, New York: Simon and Schuster.

46. Reid, K. E. (1981); *From Character Building to Social Treatment: The history of the use of groups in social work*, WestPoint, Conn.: Greenwood Press.

47. Richard Kraft and Mitchell Sakofs (Eds.) (1994). *The theory of experiential education* (2nd ed.). Boulder, CO: Association of Experiential Education.

48. Roger C. Schank (1994, October); *What we learn when we learn by doing,* Technical Report 60. Evanston, IL: Northwestern University's Institute for the Learning Sciences.

49. Schein, Edgar (1998*); Process Consultation*, Prentice Hall.

50. Schutz, W. 1958. *FIRO: A Three-Dimensional Theory of Interpersonal Behaviour.* New York: Holt, Rinehart & Winston.

51. Schein, E (1995): 'Kurt Lewin's Change Theory in the Field and in the Classroom:

52. Steiner, Claude; *Scripts People Live: Transactional Analysis of Life Scripts.* New York: Grove Press.

53. Steiner, Claude, and JoAnn Dick (illustrator); *The Original Warm Fuzzy Tale: A Fairytale.* Sacramento: Jalmar Press, 1977.

54. Stringer, E. T. (1999): Action Research 2e, Thousand Oaks, CA.: Sage.

55. Stone, J. 2006: *Managing Human Resources. Brisbane*; John Wiley and Sons Australia LTD.

56. Turquet, P.M. (1974) *Leadership: The individual and the group*, In G.S. Gibbard, J.J. Hartman and R.D. Mann (Eds.) Analysis of Groups, San Francisco: Jossey-Bass.

57. Tuckman, B. (1965); *Developmental sequence in small groups,* Psychological Bulletin, 63, 384-399.

58. Ullman, D. (2000); *Kurt Lewin: His Impact on American Psychology, or Bridging the Gorge between Theory and Reality',*

59. Webb, G. (1996); *Becoming critical of action research for development'* in O. Zuber-Skerritt (ed.) New Directions in Action Research, London: Falmer Press.

60. Wood. (2004); *Organisational Behavior: A Global Perspective.* Milton; John Wiley and Sons Australia LTD.

❑❑❑